HAROLD PINTER

Modern Critical Views

These and other titles in preparation

Modern Critical Views

HAROLD PINTER

Edited and with an introduction by

Harold Bloom
Sterling Professor of the Humanities
Yale University

CHELSEA HOUSE PUBLISHERS ◇ 1987
New York ◇ New Haven ◇ Philadelphia

Library of Congress Cataloging-in-Publication Data
Harold Pinter.
     (Modern critical views)
     Bibliography: p.
     Includes index.
     Contents: Homecoming / Bert O. States—The birthday
party / Raymond Williams—Words and silence / John
Russell Brown—[etc.]
     1. Pinter, Harold, 1930–   —Criticism and
interpretation. [1. Pinter, Harold, 1930–   —
Criticism and interpretation. 2. English drama—
History and criticism] I. Bloom, Harold. II. Series.
PR6066.I53Z666   1987   822'.914   86-29964
ISBN 0-87754-706-8 (alk. paper)

Contents

Editor's Note

This book gathers together a representative selection of the best criticism devoted to the plays of Harold Pinter. The critical essays are arranged here in the chronological order of their original publication. I am grateful to Henry Finder for his customary erudition and judgment in helping me to edit this volume.

My introduction centers upon *The Caretaker*, and seeks to uncover in it the characteristic energies of Pinter's dramatic art. The chronological sequence begins with an account of *The Homecoming* by Bert O. States, who locates in the way Pinter's personages differ from us an element he wishes to call Gothic, which would make Pinter the Poe or Huysmans of the Absurdist theatre.

The distinguished social critic, Raymond Williams, analyzes *The Birthday Party*, and sees it as the domestication in British drama of the art of Franz Kafka. In a related reading, John Russell Brown emphasizes linguistic skepticism as being a dominant mode in the same play. James Eigo, writing on *Landscape*, ponders the implications of a drama that is entirely monologue. In an exegesis of *The Room*, Austin E. Quigley puzzles out the tensions of Pinter's first play. In an overview of much of Pinter's work, Barbara Kreps sketches the metaphysics of time's enigmatic relation to this playwright's sense of possible realities. Guido Almansi, also surveying much of Pinter, emphasizes the idioms of lies, with Pinter as our guide to a land of unreliance.

Pinter's *Betrayal* is studied by Enoch Brater as a translation of cinematic images into a new theatrical idiom. Thomas F. Van Laan, analyzing *The Dumb Waiter*, centers on Pinter's play with us, the audience, in which we become active elements in the total design of the dramatic experience. In a penetrating account of parody in Pinter, Elin Diamond seeks to provide another figure in that total design.

Martin Esslin concludes this book with a meditation upon Pinter's mastery of dialogue, which is seen as a dialectic of language and silence, always crucial in this dramatist.

Introduction

Pinter is the legitimate son of Samuel Beckett, and so has a position in contemporary drama that is both assured and, perhaps more ultimately, rather difficult to sustain. *The Birthday Party, The Caretaker, The Homecoming,* and *Old Times* form an impressive panoply, but diminish, both in the study and in the theater, when brought too close to *Waiting for Godot, Endgame, Krapp's Last Tape,* plays which are after all quite certainly as enduring as *The Way of the World, The Country Wife, The School for Scandal,* and *The Importance of Being Earnest.* This is not to suggest that Pinter, at an active fifty-five, has touched his final limits, but only to admit that this most admirable of working British dramatists is shadowed by Beckett, at once his poetic father, and certainly the strongest living writer in any Western language. Aesthetically considered, the shadow of the object that falls upon Pinter's authorial ego is Beckett, who is for Pinter very much the ego ideal. A comparison of Pinter's relation to Beckett with that of Tom Stoppard to Beckett is one way of seeing how much more persuasive a literary dramatist Pinter is than Stoppard. *Rosencrantz and Guildenstern Are Dead* is a weak misreading, though a charming one, of *Waiting for Godot,* but *The Caretaker* is a strong misreading or creative interpretation of *Endgame.*

Pinter writes of the open wound, and through him, we know it open and know it closed. We tell when it ceases to beat, and tell it at its highest peak of fever. I have plagiarized those last two sentences from Pinter, substituting "Pinter" for "Shakespeare." As an insight into Shakespeare, it hardly exists, and would be almost as inadequate if I had substituted "Beckett." But it does very well for Pinter, except that he cannot close any wound whatsoever. His art has some undefined but palpable relation to the Holocaust, inevitable for a sensitive dramatist, a third of whose people were murdered before he was fifteen. A horror of violence, with an obsessive sense of the open wound, is Pinter's unspoken first principle. Whether such an implicit principle of being can sustain the most eminent drama is open to considerable question, because the stance of a conscientious objector is, in itself, by no means dramatic. Barely repressed violence, internal or external, is necessarily the Pinteresque mode, but repression, a powerful aid to the poetic Sublime, is not a defense that enchances drama.

Pinter began as a poet, rather a bad one, Eliotic and uncertain: " . . . and here am I,/Straddled, exile always in one Whitbread Ale town,/Or such./ Where we went to the yellow pub, cramped in an alley bin,/a shout from the market." That is "Gerontion" ironically transformed into an East End of London Jewish vision, and reminds one of how much more effectively Beckett ironically transforms "Gerontion" in his superb Cartesian poem, *Whoroscope*. Pinter's rhetorical art in his best plays has the same close relation to Beckett's language that the early poems have to Eliot's diction, except that Pinter does far better in the plays at assimilating the precursor's style to an idiom recognizably the latecomer's own.

A clear aid to Pinter in his accommodation of Beckett is the hidden reliance upon a very different tradition than Beckett's Anglo-Irish literary ancestry. Beckett is a kind of Gnostic, religiously speaking, though a Gnostic with a Protestant sensibility. In contrast, Pinter has definite if veiled connections to the West's oldest normative tradition, which is not exactly Gnostic, despite Gershom Scholem's sly efforts to make it so. I am suggesting that, in American Jewish literary terms, Pinter has more authentic affinities with such novelists as Philip Roth and Harold Brodkey than with the greater, menacing and quite Gnostic Nathanael West. The cosmos of Beckett's plays is what the Gnostics called the *kenoma*, the emptiness into which we have been thrown by a catastrophe-creation. Implicit in the world of Pinter's dramas, however remote, however hopelessly inaccessible, are the normative values of the Jewish tradition: rational, humane, trusting in justice and the Covenant, naturalistic without being idolatrous, and at the last hopeful, above all hopeful.

II

The Caretaker, Pinter's first success, remains a disturbing play after a quarter-century, but rereading it is a distinctly mixed aesthetic experience. A great set-piece for three virtuoso actors, its rewards for a reader deep in Kafka and Beckett necessarily are equivocal. Davies, who loses his chance to be caretaker, and goes back to his exile in the urban wilderness, is clearly a wanderer in the Kafkan and Beckettian *kenoma*, the cosmic emptiness ruled by the Archons of lies, racial hatreds, false prides, selfishnesses. That is the only universe in which Davies could be naturalized, and yet that is not the world of *The Caretaker*. Pinter's originality in the play consists in taking two nihilists—Davies and the enigmatic Mick—and one normative if damaged consciousness—Aston—and placing them together in a room that suggests a catastrophic world, smashed by a Creation-Fall, but that actually represents things as they are, our given existence, in which there can be hope even for us. In Kafka's vision there is hope, but not for us. Beckett sees no hope, apart from us, but then sees also that we have no hope. Pinter's Aston has hope, invests it in the wretched Davies, type of the natural man, and finds that the hope is betrayed. But even a betrayed hope remains a hope.

Pinter evidently first intended to end *The Caretaker* with the ambivalent brothers, Mick and Aston, combining to murder Davies in what might almost have been a parody of the Primal History Scene in Freud's *Totem and Taboo*. Martin Esslin usefully finds in Davies a kind of father archetype for Aston, and rather more precariously, for Mick as well. Aston's last words in the play, rejecting Davies, have the ironic familial reverberation of the son returning his father's complaints upon him: "You make too much noise." On Aston's part, the rest is silence, while Davies stumbles through a Pinteresque lyric of evanescense:

ASTON *moves to the window and stands with his back to* DAVIES.
> You mean you're throwing me out? You can't do that.
> Listen man, listen man, I don't mind, you see, I don't
> mind, I'll stay, I don't mind, I'll tell you what, if you
> don't want to change beds, we'll keep it as it is, I'll stay in
> the same bed, maybe if I can get a stronger piece of
> sacking, like, to go over the window, keep out the
> draught, that'll do it, what do you say, we'll keep it
> as it is?
> *Pause.*

ASTON: No.

DAVIES: Why . . . not?
> ASTON *turns to look at him.*

ASTON: You make too much noise.

DAVIES: But . . . but . . . look . . . listen . . . listen here . . . I
> mean . . .
> ASTON *turns back to the window.*
> What am I going to do?
> *Pause.*
> What shall I do?

Pause.
Where am I going to go?
Pause.
If you want me to go . . . I'll go. You just say the word.
Pause.
I'll tell you what though . . . them shoes . . . them shoes
you give me . . . they're working out all right . . . they're
all right. Maybe I could . . . get down. . . .
ASTON *remains still, his back to him, at the window.*
Listen . . . if I . . . got down . . . if I was to . . . get my
papers . . . would you . . . would you let . . . would you
. . . if I got down . . . and got my . . .
Long silence

Curtain.

The poignant, silent, normative level in Pinter's lyricism implies that
Davies is lost because he can only get his references by indeed getting down
and getting some truth, compassionate love, legitimate pride, selflessness.
That is humanly moving, but not aesthetically cogent, since the stigmata of
Beckett's *Endgame* never abandon Davies. There are no original virtues available for Davies; what makes him a persuasive representation also excludes
any possibility of his redemption. Pinter's longing for the wholesomeness
he cannot represent is, in itself, not an aesthetic longing. Davies, though the
most memorable figure in the *The Caretaker*, is also the flaw in the drama.

Pinter writes tragicomedy, and Davies, properly played, is very funny,
but this is the humor more of Kafka and his circle than it is of the relatively
genial Beckett. Aston is not funny, and Mick's comedy is deliberately cruel, .
as in a first harangue at Davies:

MICK: Jen . . . kins.
A drip sounds in the bucket. DAVIES *looks up.*
You remind me of my uncle's brother. He was always on
the move, that man. Never without his passport. Had an
eye for the girls. Very much your build. Bit of an athlete.
Longjump specialist. He had a habit of demonstrating
different run-ups in the drawing-room round about
Christmas time. Had a penchant for nuts. That's what it
was. Nothing else but a penchant. Couldn't eat enough of
them. Peanuts, walnuts, brazil nuts, monkey nuts,
wouldn't touch a piece of fruit cake. Had a marvellous
stop-watch. Picked it up in Hong Kong. The day after

they chucked him out of the Salvation Army. Used to go
in number four for Beckenham Reserves. That was before
he got his Gold Medal. Had a funny habit of carrying his
fiddle on his back. Like a papoose. I think there was a bit
of the Red Indian in him. To be honest, I've never made
out how he came to be my uncle's brother. I've often
thought that maybe it was the other way round. I mean
that my uncle was his brother and he was my uncle. But I
never called him uncle. As a matter of fact I called him
Sid. My mother called him Sid too. It was a funny
business. Your spitting image he was. Married a
Chinaman and went to Jamaica.

This marvelous fellow—who may have been Mick's and Aston's other-
wise forgotten real father—has considerably more gusto than the three characters in the play, taken together. The nut-eating Sid, long-jump specialist
with a fiddle upon his back, is a kind of Chagallian wandering Jew. Mick
ambiguously finds in Davies the exact image of Sid, towards whom an
authentic ambivalence is expressed in this fine outburst, at once admiring
and profoundly resentful. All that we can say with some assurance about
Mick is that he is playing the part of himself, without in any way being that
part, or being himself. We can surmise Mick's dialectical attitudes toward
Davies, but they are minor compared to what Pinter will not let us surmise:
What is the quality of Mick's acceptance and rejection of Aston, his brother?

Aston, rather than Davies or even Mick, seems to me the figure who is
the play's strongest representation, and in some sense can be called Pinter's
own image of voice. Damaged by the hideous shamans of our society, the
psychiatrists who are the authentic incompetents and irresponsibles among
us, Aston remains for Pinter the barely articulate hope of kindness, of a
quest for the only Western image that does not partake either of origins or
ends, the image of the father. That Aston is self-deceived into finding the
image in the unworthy Davies is hardly a fault, when we recall Mick's
association of Davies with the familial Sid. Whatever poetry Pinter feels
privileged to bring onto the stage he invests in Aston. The sadness of that
investment is humanly clear enough, but so is the aesthetic dignity that
Pinter nearly achieves, and in so unlikely a context.

BERT O. STATES

Pinter's Homecoming:
The Shock of Nonrecognition

TEDDY: *You wouldn't understand my works. You wouldn't have the faintest
idea of what they were about. You wouldn't appreciate the points of reference.
You're way behind. All of you. There's no point in my sending you my works.
You'd be lost. It's nothing to do with the question of intelligence. It's a way of
being able to look at the world. It's a question of how far you can operate on
things and not in things. I mean it's a question of your capacity to ally the
two, to relate the two, to balance the two. To see, to be able to see! I'm the
one who can see. That's why I can write my critical works. Might do you
good . . . have a look at them . . . see how certain people can view . . .
things . . . how certain people can maintain . . . intellectual equilibrium.
Intellectual equilibrium. You're just objects. You just . . . move about. I can
observe it. I can see what you do. It's the same as I do. But you're lost in it.
You won't get me being . . . I won't be lost in it.*
                    BLACKOUT.

                                    —*The Homecoming*

I want to consider this play on what seems to me its most interesting level:
that is, as a fiction about a group of people so *different* from us, while in
certain obvious respects resembling us, that they are fascinating to watch.
As a start, I propose to explore my recognition of the play in this speech
which strikes me as being *there* in a peculiar way. It is, first, what we may
call a genuine idea in a play that contains almost no ideas at all. Moreover,
it is the only place in the play where Pinter permits a character to be
undevious, "forthcoming" as Lenny would say, and that is a privilege most

From *The Hudson Review* 21, no. 3 (Autumn 1968). © 1968 by The Hudson Review,
Inc.

Pinter characters never get. Finally, as the penultimate break in the play, it is spoken with an almost thematic inflection. In fact, in the early throes of Critic's Rapture, I wondered whether Pinter wasn't very deliberately telling us more about his *Homecoming* here than about Teddy's.

Basically, the speech is Pinter's only pass at motivating Teddy's unusual capacity to "observe" with "equilibrium" the degeneration (or more correctly, the re-degeneration) of his wife to the level of his family. Applying it with a little imagination to *the rest* of Teddy, moreover, we can arrive at a coherent explanation for all of his actions: why he married a girl like Ruth, why he risked stopping off here en route back to the Campus from Venice, why he is willing (anxious, if you like) to return to the children without their mother, thus living out the pattern of his father's luck with Jessie. You can even predict, come twenty years, what intellectual barbarians the children will be, the eldest perhaps coming to a bad end in some dark form of father rejection. A New York psychoanalyst has suggested that Teddy is an example of a "totally withdrawn libido" troubled by a basic hatred for women and a tendency toward homosexuality (a family problem); he therefore substitutes intellectual equilibrium for a proper sex life. Michael Craig, who played Teddy, says he is the most violent of all the brothers, a veritable "Eichmann" underneath who has "rationalized his aggressions." Pinter, with characteristic simplicity (if not pure disinterest), says he walks out in the end to avoid a "messy fight," and anyway his marriage was on the rocks. All of these ideas (see *Saturday Review*, April 8, 1967) do not arise from the speech alone, of course, but the speech authorizes them; it puts the lid, so to speak, on Teddy's possibilities.

My feeling is that it is more a case of the play's not contradicting such ideas than of its actually containing them. Here is the one example of character "psychology" we get in the whole play and it directs us toward nothing definite in the character's experience but rather toward his *way of dealing* with whatever *happens* to be in his experience. In this respect, the speech bears out an impression confirmed by the rest of the play: the Pinter character's complete lack of interest in "things," in obligations, social or moral transactions, past "sins," future "goals," the whole world of palpable reality which Pinter is paradoxically so good at evoking in his dialogue; and his obsession with "points of reference," means, style, what can be *made* out of what is passing at any particular moment. In short, Teddy's philosophy of equilibrium is simply a more academic page out of the old family album.

In a more general sense, this helps to account for the powerful impression of the play's having been spun outward from an invisible center of complicity which clearly beckons the Interpreter to try his hand at supplying objective correlatives. On one hand, therefore, we explain the play as a study in psychic ambiguity: under the banal surface a massive Oedipal syndrome (like the part of the iceberg you can't see) bumps its way to grisly fulfillment. Or, beneath Freud lurks Jung and the archetypal: the father-sons "contest," the "fertility rite" on the sofa, the Earth Mother "sacrifice," the tribal sharing of her body (a Sparagmos for sure), the cyclical "return," and so on. But before the play is any or all of these things, it seems to be something much different and much simpler.

Perhaps the best way to pin it down is to try to say why psychology and myth seem unsatisfactory as explanations. The trouble with them is that they bring to the fore a purposiveness which seems at odds with the nature of the imagination we are dealing with. They assume that the play is *about* these things, whereas I think they come much closer to being by-products, as we would be dealing with by-products of, say, a story by Poe in the themes of crime-does-not-pay, or man-is-evil, or even in the mythic structures which I am sure there are plenty of in Poe, as there always are in tales of victimization. As for the psychological drives themselves, one somehow doubts that Pinter's characters, deep down, are any more troubled by appetites of the sexual kind than Dostoyevski's people are troubled by finding suitable jobs. They seem far more interested in manipulating the idea of sexuality, for its effect on others, than in their own performance. As for the mythic elements, it is simply hard to see what they prove, other than that Pinter deals in some pretty raw urges, hardly a distinction these days. To be "primitive" is not to be Pinteresque.

I suggest that it is in the peculiar way the story is told and in the liberties it takes with the reality it posits. For instance, if we reduce the play to its main turns of plot we have something like this: a son and his wife return to the family home on a visit abroad. Almost immediately, the father and brothers make open advances on the wife. She seems to tolerate, if not encourage, them and the husband makes no effort to protect his interests. In fact, it is the husband in the end who makes the family's proposal to the wife that she stay on as mother, mistress to everybody, and as prostitute. She accepts (!) and he goes back to their three children. We anticipate that it will be the wife who now controls the family.

It would be hard to conceive an action, in modern "family" terms, which violates so many of our moral scruples with so little effort and so little interest in making itself credible. You may read causes *into* it, but the causes pale beside the facts, like the page of repentance at the end of a dirty book. The whole thing has about it a blatant improbability and artifice which depends not upon our sympathizing, or understanding its origins, but upon our seeing how far it has taken its own possibilites. Moreover, it is all so harmless. As Eliot said of Ford's incest, the fact that such outrageous vices are defended by no one lends a color of inoffensiveness to their use. At any rate, the reaction one has to the play comes nowhere near Pity and Fear, or any of their weaker derivatives, but is better described as *astonishment at the elaboration*. And it is precisely this quality of astonishment that is apt to disappear from any thematically oriented recovery of the play.

So the idea I want to develop here is that *The Homecoming* may be about homecomings of all kinds but it is not ultimately about ours. We witness it, it even coaxes us to grope for connections among our own realities (and find them), but it does not, as its primary artistic mission, refer us back to a cluster of moral or existential issues we are very much about. What astonishes about the play is its taking of an extraordinarily brutal action, passing it through what is perhaps the most unobtrusive and "objective" medium since Chekhov's, and using it as the host for a peculiar activity of mind. We have invented special words for this activity ("Pintercourse," "Pinterism," "Pinterotic," etc.), which Pinter understandably detests, but it seems we have needed them as semantic consolation for his having hidden from us the thing they refer to.

And it is, I think, a thing—something all the characters *do* (in this play at least), with varying degrees of genius. To come back to my epigraph, what attracted me to Teddy's "philosophy" is that it offers the best explanation of this thing Pinter has given us. It is not particularly recondite, or mysterious; in fact, it goes under the household label of Irony, or the making of ironies, the art of being superior to things by disposing of them without passion or involvement. The best way to make the connection is to set Teddy's speech against this more clinical description of the ironic temper by Haakon Chevalier:

> The Ironist is committed to the search of a more and more exterior point of view, so as to embrace all contradictions and behold the world from a point of vantage to which nothing else is superior. The indefinite extension of his field of vision to the furthest attainable reaches is implied even in the point of view of the Ironic observer of a simple human situation. The Ironic reaction is exterior to both elements of the contrast observed. And this necessarily leads to a progressive extension of the point of view. Beyond the Ironist's perception of a situation is his Ironic perception of himself Ironically perceiving the situation, etc.

Now this fits and it doesn't fit, and I am ultimately more interested in the sense in which it fits Pinter's own perspective (and he, in turn, the contemporary perspective) than in its application to specific characters. It is a gentle kind of irony M. Chevalier deals with in his book about Anatole France, whereas ours is a more subterranean variety based in cruder contrasts. But it is the same operation, in essence, and as Chevalier goes on to observe, it accompanies a peculiar relationship to "everyday reality" and is "stimulated and encouraged to expression in a special environment." If you wish to think of it as the collective "motive" of the characters, and get your psychology in that way, it would certainly do no harm; but I think it has more aesthetic ramifications. For it seems to me that character is here usurping—rather wholesale—a privilege that has traditionally belonged to the audience (superiority to the situation) and that when irony is practiced to this degree of exclusiveness it might more properly be considered as a form of *audience* psychology designed by the author to meet the expectations of the "special environment" in which he writes, more about which later. This, in my opinion, is the source of our consternation and fascination with Pinter—our quest for the lost superiority of knowing more than the characters who now know more than we do, the very reverse of the familiar "dramatic" irony in which *we* know but they don't. To put it crudely, it is the goal of the Pinter character, as agent of this author's grand strategy, to stay ahead of the audience by "inventing" his drama out of the sometimes slender life afforded him (glasses of water, newspapers, cheese-rolls, etc.). His motto, in fact, might well be Renan's remark (which I also crib from Chevalier): "The universe is a spectacle that God offers himself; let us serve the intentions of the great choroegus by contributing to render the spectacle as brilliant, as varied as possible." To this end, he becomes, as it were, a little Pinter, an author of irony, sent into his incredible breathing world scarce half made-up, morally, to work on the proper business of his author's trade—to "trump" life, to go it one better by going it one worse. This, I think, is what Teddy is doing in his repressed, tweedy way in escorting his wife to the rank sweat of the family bed (which she, in turn, negotiates into a still greater triumph of "perspective") with all the possession of someone passing the salt. It is a similar triumph of perspective that moves Max to take one look at his eldest son and his wife, newly arrived from Independence America, the World's Bandwagon, and call her tart, smelly scrubber, stinking pox-ridden slut, a disease, sensing with uncanny instinct that his son is, at this moment, *bigger* than the family, outside it yet condescending to "visit," that his superiority is somehow vested in this woman and that an insult in the form of an imitation (not too convincing) of moral indignation will do the trick. It is, again, another triumph that his apology for this outrage should descend to an equally ludicrous imitation of fatherly sentimentality ("You want to kiss your old father? Want a cuddle with your old father?"). And so on, through his repertoire of sudden reversals of sentiment calculated to demonstrate that his perception of a situation includes all possible positions. For instance:

> He was fond of your mother, Mac was. Very fond. He always had a good word for her.
> *Pause.*
> Mind you, she wasn't such a bad woman. Even though it made me sick just to look at her rotten stinking face, she wasn't such a bad bitch. I gave her the best bleeding years of my life, anyway.

Finally, it is the pleasure of irony that moves the play's least gifted character, Sam, to spit out the priceless secret he has been nursing for years ("MacGregor had Jessie in the back of my cab as I drove them along") at a moment so right, so symmetrical, that the beauty of it almost kills him.

Pinter's best and most continuous irony, however, arises not from situation but from language, and on this point he reminds me a good deal of Chekhov and Beckett with whom he shares powerful affinities in imagination. Putting aside their differences, I think they are ironists in the same tradition, they hold similar fascination for us, and give us, on the whole, similar critical problems. They are probably the three least discursive playwrights one could name; in fact, their silence before the questions they raise—their Socratic smile, you might say—is so extreme that it qualifies as their special *excess*, like Genet's devout immorality, Brecht's social consciousness, Pirandello's cerebration. Such detachment is very rare in the theatre because it tends to produce the sort of play Hamlet might write, one that hovers on the verge of motionlessness (a quality for which all three have been variously praised or damned). Obviously their success with such essentially undramatic materials has a good deal to do with their preoccupation with words, silence (as anti-words), and with what we might broadly call the *expressive* aspect of life. And in each case it seems to me that even language functions in an ironic way, that our interest is centered upon a tension between the words and the situation. I was interested in Richard Gilman's article on *The Homecoming* in *The New York Times* (Jan. 22, 1967) in which he said that "language can itself be dramatic, can *be* the play, not merely the means . . . etc.," a remark which Mr. Simon trounced in *The Hudson Review* (vol. 20, no. 1, Spring 1967) as intellectual cant. Now I don't think language can *be* the play any more than the medium can *be* the message, but there is something in Mr. Gilman's idea. I think he touches upon a habit of composition which

Pinter has cultivated more and more as he goes along—a habit which is, in a technical sense, analogous to Chekhov's highly controlled practice of putting language out of proportion to the "content" (the almost *elegant* expression of near-suicidal desperation), and which we find again in Beckett's insistence on putting the significant things in the guise of insignificance ("What about hanging ourselves?"). The equivalent technique in Pinter—and especially in *The Homecoming* where it reaches a kind of *tour de force* intensity—is a direct and almost satirical formalism of expression which is, putting it mildly, inappropriate to the situation. The whole technique might be presampled in a remark Pinter himself recently made to a *Paris Review* reporter about politicians:

> I'll tell you what I really think about politicans. The other night I watched some politicians on television talking about Vietnam. I wanted very much to burst through the screen with a flame-thrower and burn their eyes out and their balls off and then inquire from them how they would assess this action from a political point of view.

I checked this on first reading because it was so interesting to see Pinter being, as it were, Pinteresque on a *real* issue he obviously felt strongly about, brilliantly satirizing the politician's habit of converting ugly reality to pure rhetoric—an almost perfect description of what he is doing in *The Homecoming*. Listen to this same politician's language now in the mouths of Max and Lenny:

> SAM: . . . you know what he said to me? He told me I was the
> best chauffeur he'd ever had. The best one.
> MAX: From what point of view?
> SAM: Eh?
> MAX: From what point of view?
> LENNY: From the point of view of his driving, Dad, and his
> general sense of courtesy, I should say.

Or this passage taken from the family discussion of how Ruth is to be treated in her "various" roles:

> MAX: Lenny, do you mind if I make a little comment? It's not
> meant to be critical. But I think you're concentrating too
> much on the economic considerations. There are other
> considerations. There are human considerations. You
> understand what I mean? There are the human
> considerations. Don't forget them.

Or take the peripety itself, in which the play arrives at its greatest gulf between manner and matter, a small masterpiece of collective one-upmanship:

> TEDDY: Ruth . . . the family have invited you to stay for a little
>   while longer. As a . . . a kind of guest. If you like the
>   idea I don't mind. We can manage very easily at home
>   . . . until you come back.
> RUTH: How very nice of them.
>   *Pause.*
> MAX: It's an offer from our heart.
> RUTH: It's very sweet of you.
> MAX: Listen . . . it would be our pleasure.

Altogether, it is an irony that disappears at times into pure comedy, reminding one of that old cartoon about the cannibal sporting the bowler and umbrella of the English gentlemen he is about to eat.

Perhaps the most spectacular example of Pinter brutality to date is the scene in which Lenny recites his deeds to Ruth, his brother's wife (whom he has known less than five minutes):

> Well, this lady was very insistent and started taking liberties with
> me down under this arch, liberties which by any criterion I
> couldn't be expected to tolerate, the facts being what they were,
> so I clumped her one. It was on my mind at the time to do away
> with her, you know, to kill her, and the fact is, that as killings
> go, it would have been a simple matter, nothing to it. Her chauf-
> feur, who had located me for her, he'd popped round the corner
> to have a drink, which just left this lady and myself, you see,
> alone, standing underneath this arch, watching all the steamers
> steaming up, no one about, all quiet on the Western Front, and
> there she was up against this wall—well, just sliding down the
> wall, following the blow I'd given her. Well, to sum up, every-
> thing was in my favour, for a killing. Don't worry about the
> chauffeur. The chauffeur would never have spoken. He was an
> old friend of the family. But . . . in the end I thought . . . Aaah,
> why go to all the bother . . . you know, getting rid of the corpse
> and all that, getting yourself into a state of tension. So I just gave
> her another belt in the nose and a couple of turns of the boot and
> sort of left it at that.

Now there is a serious question here as to whether Lenny really did this at all, much less with such terrifying indifference; but that is beside the point, just as it is beside the point to inquire whether the family is capable of having sex with Ruth. The main thing is the conception and framing of the possibility, the something *done* to the brutality that counts. The genial minimization of it, you might say. And Lenny accomplishes this by satirizing his act in the language his "betters" habitually use to sanitize themselves from dockside realities of just this sort. The effect, of course, is to make him superior to his brutality, to the class morality he is mimicking, and to his freshest opponent in what his soul-brother Mick, in the *The Caretaker*, calls "the game." In a sense I think the actor will appreciate, life is *all* performance for Lenny, a veritable charade of politesse.

The question is, what does it mean to an audience? Is Pinter our Molière of the bullock-pen? Is he saying that insofar as language is supposed to correspond to deed and intent it is being "spilled," and the entire moral structure along with it? That the Family is taking out its spite against society by imitating it to its own "diseased" specifications (each character being an aspect of, first English, then "modern" decay), and that in order to avoid such corruption as theirs, as one critic has pointed out, we have got to pull together somehow, wake up to our encroaching dehumanization? Or, what seems a more commonly held view, that the play is simply descriptive of a condition we can do nothing about, given the persistence of the beast in the genes, but which it is the artist's instinct and duty to portray, in the belief that an aesthetic triumph over life is better than none at all? In short, what does the presence of such Irony, as the very *process* of the play, signify on our scene?

In the *Paris Review* article, Pinter was asked if he considered the world "an essentially violent place." Yes, it was violent all right, he said, but the violence was "really only an expression of the question of dominance and subservience," the repeated theme (he thought) of his plays. There is about Pinter's remarks on himself a very refreshing sense of the craftsman in his shop (or rather, *out* of it, and wanting to get back), and none of the displaced philosopher taking his chance to talk (art being mute). All questions, if possible, are converted to matters of technique—*"writing the bloody play!"* In his remark I think he has converted our world into his own artistic frame of reference very thoroughly: a question of dominance and subservience, a "common everyday thing." Reflecting it against the plays, the telling thing about it is its fixation on *the fact* of violence as a kind of source, or quarry to be mined, and its unconcern for the consequences of violence on the human scene. Does it not, in fact, bespeak a certain detachment that comes with accommodation to, or indifference toward, an "old" problem?

Now one might easily invoke here Chekhov's famous comeback to the accusation of indifference—"We don't have to be *told* that stealing horses is bad." In other words, the objective, no-comment depiction of malevolence carries its own power of denial and opposition, its own unfurled sympathy with health. And it undoubtedly does—when the artist *wants* it to and sees to it that the ironies are leaned in that direction. But I have never been convinced that Chekhov wanted it to and that he was not absolutely fascinated by the blackest possibilities of the void out of which Shestov said he created. Moreover, questions of this sort occur: Do we not underestimate the attractiveness of evil? Is not one of the pleasures of art evil's power to arrest for our delight certain hold lines of force which goodness simply doesn't possess? To bring it up to date, could we not be arriving at a kind of art (of which Pinter is our most daring example) which is showing signs of restlessness with its content and is therefore shifting its focus from an attention to the content for its own sake (our Absurd "condition") to the interesting symmetries inherent in it?

I seem to be suggesting that Pinter is callously producing what Mr. Wimsatt calls "vile art," art which presents immoral acts irresponsibly, if not with approval and joy (as we are told our movies are doing these days). I am not really prepared to argue that question; but I feel obliged to put Pinter into the context he deserves most and that amounts to considering him as a craftsman rather than a thinker, a maker of theatre out of "accepted" materials. In short, I find the question of whether he sees the world as "essentially violent" about as interesting and relevant to his art as whether, let us say, John Constable sees the world as essentially peaceful. And I would enlarge this idea along the following line:

It would appear that Absurdist violence, like all forms of radical experience "used" and then "used up" by artists, may be passing into its twilight or "aesthetic" stage and that our reactions to it are changing in subtle and remarkable ways, impossible to assess. We know very little about this strange passage in the arts in which moral actions figure powerfully as the context, but we are learning something about how greatly it influences the course of the graphic arts; and there seems no reason to exempt the drama from the implications of Wöfflin's well-known idea that paintings owe more to other paintings than they owe to nature; nor from E. H. Gombrich's more recent expansion of that general idea that it is "the power of expectation rather than the power of conceptual knowledge that molds what we see in life no less than in art." We see reality, in other words, in terms of our formulations of it.

It is not appropriate to develop this far-ranging idea in very great detail here, but one of the ways in which the power of expectation would seem to operate on the dramatic artist is in adjusting his field of vision between "what has been done," to put it simply, and "what is left to do," or, if you prefer, between the images of other artists (in and out of his medium) and the suggestions they carry for further expansion. Since violence is the natural content of all "serious" drama, it seems reasonable to assume that violence (to personify it) goes a progress through the available possibilities in a constant struggle to recapture its power of fascination; one of the ways it appears to do this, as I trust the history of drama will show, is to take daring permissions with its inherited conceptions of itself, to become by turns more particular, more inward, more subtle, more "free," more "immoral," more "real," more indifferent, more sophisticated, more paradoxical (a standard device for eluding discovery); to parody itself, to offer as much sensation as the traffic will bear, and so on, until it is finally performing with only a side glance at Nature herself, the reality observed being mainly the already formulated realities of the tradition to which it belongs. Fidelity to experience, moral qualm, truth, these are indeed perpetuated, but in the terms of the medium. Something of this sort seems to have been happening in the later Greek plays (*Orestes* comes to mind) and again in those chain-reactive monstrosities of lust and cruelty of the Jacobeans—the sort of plays, in other words, which our theatre is rapidly discovering as "surprisingly playable" and which critics are busy writing down as remarkable prefigurations of the existential view of life, or—if not that—as clear proofs of the author's disillusion with his age.

To what extent all this is reflective of external changes in moral patterns and tolerances it is probably not possible to say; certainly the interplay is greater than I am suggesting in this one-sided presentation and I am stating the whole case badly in forcing a separation of the insoluble marriage of Morals and Aesthetics. But it does seem to me that the incidence of irony on our scene (and I have discussed only one particular, if not rare, variety)—which has led Northrop Frye and others to conclude that irony is the characteristic fictional mode of our century—might be reckoned in our criticism as a somewhat less depressing thing than our loss of spiritual security. Does it not open also the possibility of irony's appeal as a form of more or less pure patterning, of the manipulation of "experience" into certain kinds of symmetries (the predictable operation of dissonance) which the mind finds innately interesting because (1) it appreciates symmetry of any kind, irrespective of its bearing on human ideals, and (2) at certain times in the flux of art traditions it craves the release of the ironic variation, the art, as Frye says, which has "no object but its subject" (or, as Empson says, the art which enables the artist to say "a plague on both your houses"). Thus, we might theorize that irony has two aspects: it is, in the moral sense, a defense against the failure of any single option to convince, the loss of a clear stake in an ideological inheritance; and, in the aesthetic sense, it is a defense against the exhaustion of a set of inherited images. No doubt there is an intricate relationship between the two (if *two* there are); the point I wish to make here is that in such movements there are such things as artists who are less interested in revealing us than in amazing us.

Getting back to Poe for a moment, I am reminded of a recent essay in *Kenyon Review* by Terence Martin who makes a case for Poe's "play habit," the "desire to astonish by boundless exaggeration or confusion of proportions." He is "our one author," says Mr. Martin, "who makes an absolute commitment to the imagination—who releases the imagination into a realm of its own where, with nothing to play *with*, it must play *at* our destruction. He shows us insistently that the imagination at his kind of play is not only antisocial but antihuman. To do justice to his contemporaries, perhaps we should say that what Poe undertook was not to be looked at without blinking."

That is more or less how I feel about Harold Pinter. In fact, with just a little transposing, we could probably derive most of the old Gothic essentials from our play: the nightmare setting, the double vision of the real and the superreal, the lurking fatality and inexplicable tyranny, the mysterious inspecificity and yet *utter* relevance of everything. Even—allowing for an unfortunate degeneration in our heroine—the central Gothic theme of the pale and lovely maiden *dominated* by the inscrutable sadist of the "nameless vice." This is not intended as a dismissal of either Pinter or Gothicism. If anything, it is a plug for art which produces reactions other than the shock of recognition, art in which the very limitedness of the artist to relatively outré kinds of experience and his ability to arouse the precise *sense* of that experience are the things to be praised. To me, Pinter falls brilliantly into this category and it is with considerable respect for him that I subscribe to his own evaluation of himself as "overblown tremendously" by people who "tend to make too much of a meal." This is not at all to deny the good chance that he may come out in the end as the Poe or Huysmans of the Absurdist theatre—a better fate, perhaps, than the one in store for some of our sterner moralists.

RAYMOND WILLIAMS

The Birthday Party: *Harold Pinter*

There is a point in the development of many dramatic forms when the original strangeness can be mastered, the difficult convention learned as a method, and the unusual structure of feeling assumed. The form is then available, in quite new ways, for use in the theatre.

This seems to me the essential history of Harold Pinter's plays. They are strange only in the absence of a tradition in European literature of the last fifty years. What they represent is the domestication, in an English theatrical idiom, of what had been a strange form. *The Birthday Party*, written in 1957, is an example of just this skillful adaptation. It is what had been the strange world of Kafka, now in an English seaside boarding house. The characteristic pair of attendants, the strange agents or messengers, come to break and carry away a young man. The menace of what they are doing is tangible but unexplained; it is the irruption of a bizarre and arbitrary violence into an ordinary life. The structure of feeling is familiar: the precarious hold on reality, the failures of communication, the inevitability of violence and exploitation. In drama, this world had already been realized: most evidently in Ionesco, but also in Eliot's *Sweeney Agonistes* and in Beckett. It is always in a sense recalcitrant, this world of the absurd, in which it is in the gaps between what can be said that the arbitrary action, the overwhelming preoccupation, pushes through, and in which language, across the gaps, take the form of a comic nightmare. What Pinter is able to do is to assume this structure, and to find a way of communicating it in terms of the English

From *Drama from Ibsen to Brecht*. © 1952, 1968 by Raymond Williams. Chatto & Windus Ltd. and Oxford University Press, 1971.

theatre. At the beginning of *The Birthday Party*, the philosophical absurd is already an old friend: the deck-chair attendant and his landlady wife:

> Petey?
> What?
> Is that you?
> Yes, it's me.
> What? Are you back?
> Yes.
> I've got your cornflakes ready. Here's your cornflakes. Are
>   they nice?
> Very nice.
> I thought they'd be nice.

This is the theatrical idiom of socially inarticulate people, as conventionally presented, for a kind of comedy, on the English middle-class stage. It is through this lead, in what is already a known game, that the gap is opened, and when the strange agents arrive they are also, in the first instance, familiar theatrical characters: a stage Irishman and a stage Jew. The ordinary counters, of a conventional English naturalist comedy of the lower classes and of foreigners, are used to initiate an action which in its direct terms would lack these essential connections: a known absurd calls to an unknown, and the necessary trick is turned.

What then happens, in *The Birthday Party*, is that the idiom of naturalist comedy—the deck-chair attendant, the landlady, the lodger, the tart, the Irishman, the Jew—is developed to the point where the irruption of another consciousness—a malignant universal bullying—is not, and has no need to be, an irruption into an everyday world; that acceptance has already been gained, by the conversion of ordinary life into this kind of theatre. The opportunity to show menace—an inarticulate menace—is then fully taken. The birthday party, with its drum, its switching-off of lights, its game of blind-man's bluff, releases the violence, in a further stroke of theatre. The shock of bringing together these two idioms—virtually of farce and of melodrama—is controlled by their separate, prepared familiarity. With the conventions loosened, by the theatrically acceptable evasion of probability, the central scenes of interrogation, the human breaking and bewilderment, can occur in their own terms. Names are confused, identities shuffled; miscellaneous charges, at once grave and ridiculous, are hurled in a rapid stage patter:

Why did you change your name?
I forgot the other one.
What's your name now?
Joe Soap.
You stink of sin.
I can smell it.
Do you recognize an external force?
That's the question!
Do you recognize an external force, responsible for you,
    suffering for you?
It's late.
Late! Late enough! When did you last pray?
He's sweating.
Is the number 846 possible or necessary?
Neither.
Wrong. Is the number 846 possible or necessary?
Both.
Wrong. It's necessary but not possible.
Both.
Wrong!—

It is the edge of metaphysical menace of Beckett, crossed with the terrifying platitudes of Ionesco. But the point is always the theatrical effect. The menace is of the agents of an unnamed organization, and the fact that it is unnamed allows every effect at once: criminal, political, religious, metaphysical. Behind the effects is an effective conviction, now in its turn a cliché, but there to be drawn on as an active unlocated experience: that "they" will get you— drag you back to a wife, a shop, striped trousers and black jacket, duty, respectability, death. It is Mr. Polly raised to a pseudometaphysical status; a social experience abstracted to an idiom of isolation and the breakdown of language. He is secretive and dangerous anyway; furtive as all men are furtive; the dragging to grace or to death, or simply back to striped trousers, is in a final sense indifferent.

Pinter's theatrical projection of the difficult conventions of the absurd is consistently successful, in these essentially minor ways. But his most substantial achievement is something quite different, below the conventional levels of the absurd. There was a point, in the evolution of naturalist dialogue, when the repetitions, the questionings, the dead phrases, the gaps of an accepted inarticulacy could be worked on, reduced and stylized, to a conventional idiom. Eliot worked on it, in his early comic-strip characters, and it is still there, as a style, in the first scene of *The Cocktail Party*. Pinter took this further, in the different context of ordinary English speech: a fragmentary rhythm, in a particular interest: the deluded and dangerous comedy of ordinariness; the dead strangeness and menace of a drifting, routine-haunted, available common life. It has been widely imitated, in many different forms:

> Had they heard about us, Petey?
> They must have done.
> Yes, they must have done. They must have heard this as a
>   very good boarding house. It is. This house is on the list.
> It is.
> I know it is.

What this offers is at once the attachment to ordinary life—the conviction of normality, of the everyday—and a covert valuation, beyond the anxious imitation—of a loss of significance, a loss of reality: a naturalism at once confirmed and emptied of content, given a different content; the hollow men not masked and chanting, but in ordinary clothes, speaking ordinary words; a loss of spiritual connection now at last domesticated; the strange idiom of the absurd become a theatrical method.

JOHN RUSSELL BROWN

Words and Silence: The Birthday Party

At the centre of Pinter's plays is a scepticism about language of unusual tenacity. Can anything ever be said to be stated correctly in words? Can anything ever be said to be "stated?" We play with words, and words play with us. We can neither say what we know, nor know what we say. When we stop to think, we do not trust words.

Philosophers have often warned us. In *Adventures in Ideas* (1933), Alfred North Whitehead insisted on the daring delicacy of his task:

> In the study of ideas it is necessary to remember that insistence
> on hard-headed clarity issues from sentimental feeling, as it were
> a mist, cloaking the perplexities of fact. Insistence on clarity at
> all costs is based on sheer superstition as to the mode in which
> human intelligence functions. Our reasonings grasp at straws for
> premises and float on gossamers for deductions.

This is very like the stance that Pinter took, when, early in his career, he was persuaded to talk for an hour about his work. He spoke with precise and well-timed emphasis, aware that his audience sought to pin him down:

> I'm not a theorist. I'm not an authoritative or reliable commen-
> tator on the dramatic scene, the social scene, any scene. I write
> plays, when I can manage it, and that's all. That's the sum of it.
> So I'm speaking with some reluctance, knowing that there are at
> least twenty-four possible aspects of any single statement, de-

From *Theatre Language*. © 1972 by John Russell Brown. Taplinger Publishing, 1972.

pending on where you're standing at the time or on what the
weather's like. A categorical statement, I find, will never stay
where it is and be finite. It will immediately be subject to modification by the other twenty-three possibilites of it. No statement
I make, therefore, should be interpreted as final and definitive.
One or two of them may sound final and definitive; they may
even be *almost* final and definitive; but I won't regard them as
such tomorrow and I wouldn't like you to do so today.

Awareness of the inadequacy of language can infect all social consciousness.
In a book recording his conversations, the philosopher Whitehead is shown
to be soberly aware of the inadequacy and comedy of talk:

The notion that thought can be perfectly or even adequately
expressed in verbal symbols is idiotic. . . . Take the simplest
statement of a fact: that we three are sitting in this room. Nearly
everything of importance is left out. "This room" presupposes a
building, Cambridge, the university, the world around us of
which we are a part, stellar systems of which our world is a part,
the infinite past from which we have come, and the endless future
which is streaming through us and out ahead of us. It presupposes
our separate individualities, each quite different, and all that we
know, we are, or have ever done. That verbalization of our sitting
here means next to nothing; yet, in much more serious subjects
and on a far more ambitious scale, we are constantly accepting
statements of historic fact, and philosophical speculations which
are much more lacking in accuracy or in any relationship with
exact truth. When such over-simplified ideas are addressed to
persons who cannot supply the omitted presuppositions, they
mean nothing, are not comprehended, are not even taken in.

As a dramatist Pinter explores such inadequacies of words, the presuppositions of speech and the barriers to comprehension. But he is not a destructive
investigator; he also delights in words, teases them, appears to wait for them,
and purposely avoids them. Interplay between confidence in words and fear
of them, and between what is meant and what is betrayed, is a constant
source of excitement in Pinter's stage dialogue, as if it were the life-blood
and the nerves of all his writing. His audiences are invited to listen with
precise attention and to recognize in the words—and all "around" them—a
reflection of their own attempts to make statements and communicate.

Pinter had the wit to see that difficulties in the use of words are potential dramatic capital. He has so constantly exploited what words do *not* clearly define, that he seems to have set out consciously to use the very imprecision of speech in an art that was, traditionally, all precision, composed of speeches each as fine and directly meaningful as could be. Pinter had written unpublished novels, stories and poems before turning to drama, but he found, one day, that drama was the form in which he could explore, control and share what he already had begun to sense happening within himself, and in the world which he inhabited.

His perception of the varying effectiveness of words is particularly dramatic. He is interested in speech as barriers and as bridges between people, as elements in a social combat. In the lecture already quoted, Pinter chose several metaphors from warfare—confront, hilt, overcome, smokescreen, stratagem, rearguard; others are from sickness, physical pressure, commerce, nakedness.

> I have mixed feelings about words myself. Moving among them, sorting them out, watching them appear on the page, from this I derive a considerable pleasure. But at the same time I have another strong feeling about words which amounts to nothing less than nausea. Such a weight of words confronts us, day in day out, words spoken in a context such as this, words written by me and by others, the bulk of it a stale dead terminology; ideas endlessly repeated and permutated, become platitudinous, trite, meaningless. Given this nausea, it's very easy to be overcome by it and step back into paralysis. I imagine most writers know something of this kind of paralysis. But *if it is possible to confront this nausea, to follow it to its hilt and move through it, then it is possible to say that something has occurred, that something has even been achieved.*
>
> Language, under these conditions, is a highly ambiguous commerce. So often, below the words spoken, is the thing known and unspoken. . . . You and I, the characters which grow on a page, most of the time we're inexpressive, giving little away, unreliable, elusive, evasive, obstructive, unwilling. But it's out of these attributes that a language arises. *A language*, I repeat, *where, under what is said, another thing is being said.*

The italicized passages display the essentially dramatic qualities in Pinter's use of language: expectation of achievement, search, surprise, developing understanding. Language is a weapon that is used for exciting tactics in a series of human encounters. Speech is warfare, fought on behalf of thoughts, feelings and instincts. Speech infects and therefore informs silence, too:

> There are two silences. One when no word is spoken. The other when perhaps a torrent of language is being employed. This speech is speaking of a language locked beneath it. That is its continual reference. *The speech we hear is an indication of that we don't hear. It is a necessary avoidance, a violent, sly, anguished or mocking smokescreen which keeps the other in its place.* When true silence falls we are still left with echo but are nearer nakedness.
>
> One way of looking at speech is to say it is a constant stratagem to cover nakedness.
>
> I think that we communicate only too well, in our silence, in what is unsaid, and that what takes place is continual evasion, desperate rearguard attempts to keep ourselves to ourselves. Communication is too alarming. To enter into someone else's life is too frightening. To disclose to others the poverty within us is too fearsome a possibility.

Four years later, when an interviewer for *Paris Review* asked Pinter the bland question:

> Why do you think the conversations in your plays are so effective?

he replied briefly, and warily, but in much the same terms as he had used in this early lecture:

> I don't know, I think possibly it's because people fall back on anything they can lay their hands on verbally to keep away from the danger of knowing, and of being known.

Given that the dramatist is concerned with eventual disclosure, here, in describing his character's "conversations," Pinter touches upon the dangerous, or precarious, nature of his plays and their stunning, appalled and held (or arrested) climaxes. From the first word spoken on stage, the hunt is on. In his lecture, he continued to explain:

> I'm not suggesting that no character in a play can ever say what he in fact means. Not at all. I have found that there invariably does come a moment when this happens, where he says something, perhaps, which he has never said before. And where this happens, what he says is irrevocable, and can never be taken back.

There are obvious dangers in this approach to playwriting. How can the audience be persuaded to attend closely enough, and to wait for clarification? When can the smokescreen be permitted to cover the battle totally, how soon, and for how long? When is the time for revelation? Should it come in silence or in words? Pinter's solutions are very varied and meticulous, and reflect a penetrating understanding of how we live.

The opening of his first full-length play, *The Birthday Party* (1958), illustrates some of his simpler strategies:

The living-room of a house in a seaside town. A door leading to the hall down left. Back door and small window up left. Kitchen hatch, centre back. Kitchen door, up right. Table and chairs, centre.

> PETEY *enters from the door on the left with a paper and sits at the table. He begins to read.* MEG's *voice comes through the kitchen hatch.*

MEG: Is that you, Petey?

> *Pause.*

Petey, is that you?

> *Pause.*

Petey?

PETEY: What?

MEG: Is that you?

PETEY: Yes, it's me.

MEG: What? *Her face appears at the hatch.* Are you back?

PETEY: Yes.

MEG: I've got your cornflakes ready. *She disappears and reappears.* Here's your cornflakes.

> *He rises and takes the plate from her, sits at the table, props up the paper and begins to eat.* MEG *enters by the kitchen door.*

Are they nice?

PETEY: Very nice.

MEG: I thought they'd be nice. *She sits at the table.* You got your paper?

PETEY: Yes.

MEG: Is it good?

PETEY: Not bad.

MEG: What does it say?

PETEY: Nothing much.

MEG: You read me out some nice bits yesterday.

PETEY: Yes, well, I haven't finished this one yet.

MEG: Will you tell me when you come to something good?
PETEY: Yes.
  Pause.
MEG: Have you been working hard this morning?
PETEY: No. Just stacked a few of the old chairs. Cleaned up a
  bit.
MEG: Is it nice out?
PETEY: Very nice.
  Pause.
MEG: Is Stanley up yet?
PETEY: I don't know. Is he?
MEG: I don't know. I haven't seen him down yet.
PETEY: Well then, he can't be up.
MEG: Haven't you seen him down?
PETEY: I've only just come in.
MEG: He must be still asleep.
  *She looks round the room, stands, goes to the sideboard and takes
  a pair of socks from a drawer, collects wool and a needle and goes
  back to the table.*
  What time did you go out this morning, Petey?
PETEY: Same time as usual.
MEG: Was it dark?
PETEY: No, it was light.
MEG *beginning to darn*: But sometimes you go out in the
  morning and it's dark.
PETEY: That's in the winter.
MEG: Oh, in winter.
PETEY: Yes, it gets light later in winter.
MEG: Oh.
  Pause.
  What are you reading?

The play starts with silence; if this is held for a moment, the audience
will wait for Petey to speak. But Pinter breaks the silence with words from
an unseen source, so gathering a further curiosity. After "Is that you, Petey?"
a pause repeats the exploitation of theatrical vacuum and still further develops
the audience's desire for it to be filled. Pinter does not let go of this tension
until line 6, with Petey's "Yes, it's me," and then Meg appears on stage.

He is not merely withholding information, for the repetitions of words
have been carefully judged. This is, indeed, a basic device in all the plays.

Meg's first three questions seem at first to repeat the same inquiry, but the slight changes in the use of words reveal progressively that the questions she asks are not truly questions at all, but a challenge. "Petey" is placed first at the end of the sentence, then more commandingly at the beginning, and then becomes the single questioning word. Moreover, when Petey's voice gives sufficient answer, three more questions follow at once, repeating the ostensible inquiry. Meg is not satisfied until she *sees* Petey, and then she herself responds with an assertion that she has done a job for him. At this point she breaks contact to bring the cornflakes to the kitchen hatch, and this action will make him rise from the table, go to her, and take them from her. Her questions, statements and action all establish that she is calling the tune; she wishes to make him acknowledge her presence and his dependence.

Other repetitions in this passage still further suggest the drama underneath the seemingly inconsequential exchanges. Petey starts by evading any statement—"What?"—but his second speech begins with "Yes," as if he were intent on cutting off the exchange. He continues, however, with "it's me," a repetition of the information given in "Yes" that is unnecessary and therefore seems insistent or, more likely, irritated or mocking. Petey's third speech defines more closely his desire to disengage by repeating for the third time the essential message with a second "Yes," which now, in contrast with his previous speech, sounds brief, uninviting and yet, possibly, submissive.

Meg's first entrance on to the stage itself and the preceding pause will gain the audience's attention for her "Are they nice?" If the audience has begun to question the validity of speech, it may consider that cornflakes are not likely to vary in themselves and therefore her question may sound like a challenge, asking for attention or praise, rather than a genuine inquiry. The repetition of "nice" in her next response—"I thought they'd be nice"—shows that this interpretation is correct, and because this speech adds nothing substantial to the exposition the audience is more likely to become at least partly aware of her pursuit of gratification.

During these speeches Petey is hidden behind the "propped up" newspaper, but now Meg challenges this protection with a further question which is now—and the contrast with earlier exchanges will make this point more clearly—overtly a challenge: "You got your paper?" Then the attack implicit in "Are they nice?" is repeated in her "Is it good?" and the similarity again helps to define the point. A *Pause* is now repeated, followed by a new question, this time more apparently concerned for Petey, as if she were recognizing—without ever saying so—that he has not been satisfying the needs which have launched her upon the whole conversation and make her, instinctively, prolong it: "Have you been working hard this morning?" But as soon as he answers with rather more detail than he has given in earlier exchanges, she accepts the small victory, and now the repetition of "nice" signals a reversion to her basic, selfish concerns. After the next *Pause*, these particular repetitions momentarily cease; this in itself suggests a shift of engagement and throws the new questions about Stanley into relief. But then there follows another *Pause* in which Meg looks and moves around the room and gets some darning to do; settled again, she tries another inquiry— "What time did you go out this morning, Petey?" This reverts to the more personal challenge of Petey and leads to another question which in form is like "Is it nice?" or "Is it good?" but this time, there is an unexpected "Was it dark?" This could be a far-reaching modification, expressing fear and apprehension; and it stands out as the first directly affecting word in the play. Now, for the first time, she seems to question his response, and she then repeats *his* words—"Oh, in winter"—and then she repeats merely her own ejaculation of acceptance or reassurance: "Oh." Satisfaction is restored in the pause, for she returns to the earlier, challenging question in a less avoidable form, not "What does it say?" but "What are you reading?"

Petey's speeches are as full of repetitions as Meg's. "Yes" is common, and it is noticeable that when it comes for the last time, in "Yes, it gets light later in winter," it comes without prompting from a question. At this point it is an attack rather than an evasion. Three times he simply repeats Meg's words or phrasing:

> Is that you? . . . Yes, it's me.
> Are they nice? . . . Very nice.
> Is it nice out? . . . Very nice.

And with as little disturbance of the phrasing, he parries or contradicts her:

> Is it good? . . . Not bad.
> Was it dark? . . . No, it was light.

Petey is disclosing as little as possible, protecting himself, holding himself still; yet he is rather furtively ready to take small advantages.

The passage about Stanley is different from the other exchanges. To Meg's first question, "Is Stanley up yet?" Petey answers briefly—"I don't know"—but he adds a question: "Is he?" Other than his first defensive "What?" this is his only question in the episode, and it provokes Meg to a repetition of his words, and then a statement of her own knowledge which sounds like an excuse: "I don't know. I haven't seen him down yet." Now Petey takes advantage and almost attacks—"Well then, he can't be up." Now Meg asks an obvious question and gets the obvious answer; and then she concludes with a further obvious statement or excuse. Here the repetitions show questions unnecessarily asked and statements unnecessarily made: Meg goes on, it must seem, because of the subject and because she is apologetic, not because she cannot work matters out for herself.

The repetitions, the disproportions, the easy use of "nice," "good" and "bad," are all occasions for comedy. So are the movements underneath the dialogue as shown by these devices. But, more than this, the two characters are at work with sly, mocking, perhaps anguished, smokescreens. There is "continual evasion"; even in attack, as little as possible is given away.

The device of repetition, so prevalent here, is not, of course, Pinter's own discovery. It is the stock-in-trade of oratory, comedy and drama, and of all speech. But Pinter uses it with astonishing persistence, repeating the simplest phrases until they yield the secret of their character's hidden activity.

Two analogies offer themselves. First Shakespeare's comic usage, as in Sir Andrew Aguecheek's first entry in *Twelfth Night*, when the foolish knight is forced to repeat his opening greetings to Sir Toby and Maria who are there to mock him. Even his first line, "Sir Toby Belch! How now, Sir Toby Belch?" is capable of being delivered with a marked change in the repeated words which could serve an experienced comic actor to establish Sir Andrew's motives and expectations as clearly as many complicated words. In the soliloquies of Benedick or Falstaff, small repetitions, often of apparently simple words such as "I am well" and "I'll never," or "Honour" and "a word," mark the climaxes and changing intentions of the speakers. Such repetitions are all the more effective in terms of character presentation and involvement because they involve words that sound at first unremarkable or casual. The dramatist, through repetition, has flogged life into a dead horse.

Secondly, Eugene O'Neill's use of repetition in his last plays, especially in *Long Day's Journey into Night*. The repeated phrase of Tyrone, "I'm as hungry as a hunter," shows how tired metaphors and mere commonplaces can become at last alive with personal and precise meaning. The phrases become a kind of pillory or cross on which the characters have unwittingly impaled their inward selves. Meg's use of "nice" and "good," and later of "lovely," are phrases that catch their user in this way.

The dramatic tactic of repetition is a surprisingly neat mechanism. By placing a short series of similar verbal utterances side by side, the audience's attention is drawn to the dissimilarities. By breaking the series, a change of direction will register more surely. Obviously this tactic needs tact in application: too long a series will weary the audience; variations must be clearly placed, as at the beginning or end of a speech; and they must be marked by a changed rhythm. Timing must be slow if the effect is to be subtle, or there must be motionless pauses in which the changes can be noticed. (In a slow-motion film or still photograph, an athlete can discover errors which he cannot know from a film at normal speed.) Activity on stage or excitement of plot must not be allowed to distract attention from simple-seeming words. (O'Neill's plays are very long and their plots slow; Shakespeare's comic scenes are often soliloquies with little obligatory stage-business, and they often fail to forward the plot at all.) Above all, the dialogue must "ring true" to character and situation. (The hardest test for an impostor is a slow, intimate, undeflecting scrutiny.)

Pinter's strong ally in all this is the actor. Increasingly since the Second World War, actors have been trained to distinguish "text" from "subtext," to appreciate a language "where, under what is said, another thing is being said." The ultimate masters are Chekhov for practice and Stanislavski for training and precept. In *Building a Character* (translated 1949), the teacher explains that each actor must create a subtextual life for his part:

> This inner stream of images, fed by all sorts of fictional inventions, given circumstances, puts life into a role, it gives a basis for everything the character does, his ambitions, thoughts, feelings.

> It is the subtext that makes us say the words we do in a play.

> The spoken word, the text of a play is not valuable in and of itself, but is made so by the inner content of the subtext and what is contained in it. . . . Without it the words have no excuse for being presented on stage.

Pinter has said that he learnt little at the acting schools he attended before becoming an actor, but, even if this were wholly true, he could scarcely have worked in the English theatre for the last twenty years without becoming aware of the notion of "subtext."

Two exercises described by Stanislavski, and recommended by his followers, show how actors are trained to search below their lines and build their performances on secure subtextual foundations:

> If I ask you a perfectly simple question now, "Is it cold out today?" before you answer, even with a "yes," or "it's not cold," or "I didn't notice," you should, in your imagination, go back on to the street and remember how you walked or rode. You should test your sensations by remembering how the people you met were wrapped up, how they turned up their collars, how the

snow crunched underfoot, and only then can you answer my question.

After this silent preparation, an answer to the question will express the whole wintry experience, even in a simple "yes"; not explicitly of course, but implicitly. The inner response, being precise and detailed, will control the volume, speed, pitch and tone of the monosyllable. The actor needs to make such a preparation at the beginning of *The Birthday Party* when, as Petey, he has to answer questions about the weather or about his cornflakes.

A more purposeful subtextual life is suggested by an exploratory exercise described in *Building a Character*:

> "Now make this test. What response do you give to the words in your ears, 'Let's go to the station!'?"
>
> I saw myself leaving the house, taking a cab, driving through certain streets, crossing avenues and soon found myself inside the railway station. Leo thought of himself as pacing up and down a platform, whereas Sonya's thoughts had already allowed her to flit off to southern climes and visit several resorts.
>
> After each one of us had described his mental pictures to Tortsov his comment was:
>
> "Evidently the two or three words were scarcely out of my mouth before you mentally carried out the suggestion contained in them! How painstakingly you have told to me all the things my little phrase evoked. . . . If you would always go through that normal process on the stage and pronounce your words with such affection and such penetration into their essential meaning you would soon become great actors."

The point of this exercise is threefold: that each student responded according to his own cast of thought and feeling, although the teacher's words and their pronunciation were identical; that an actor must be able to create a lively imaginative consciousness to support whatever he says in a play, be that complicated or simple; that simple words can evoke extensive reactions, based on past experience and future intentions, underneath their simplest meaning. . . .

Certainly Pinter's plays need good actors. If they have not realized that his words are often smokescreens and so have not created a subtextual reality to support them, his dialogue will fall flat, his plays seem idle, trivial and often banal. Without the actors' subtextual realization of their parts, the words, as Stanislavski said, "have no excuse for being presented on the stage." And the right "inner content" must be found that is both consistent throughout the play and capable of supporting every turn of the dialogue. Pinter has not freed his actors to bring their own notions and virtuosity to their parts; as he said in an interview, "There are certain limits on the actors set by what I write: they can enjoy themselves, but not in the way that Wolfit or McMaster enjoyed enjoying themselves."

Since Pinter's plays in performance require good actors who have rehearsed with concentration and consistency, it would seem to follow that they will also need perceptive readers who are equally aware of the words as part of a number of carefully wrought and interrelated performances. But for audiences and readers, he holds much slacker reins. Close and theatrically aware reading is very rewarding, but the play can be approached at any level of understanding. Sixteen million people watched one of his plays on television in a single night, with all the various distractions to which television is subject. Undoubtedly part of the attraction of the plays to readers and audiences is that each individual is left to catch the inner reality as and when he is able or willing. It is possible to lose patience with the dialogue, thinking it baffling, uneconomic, inapposite, obvious, self-important. But there are many devices to engage attention, and very few will hear or see the plays without catching intimations of the inner drama for at least some strange and disconnected moments. On rereading or reseeing, the warfare behind the words will register with growing consistency and clarity.

Talking of his characters and their speech, Pinter uses words like "true," "necessary," "firmly based"; he asks "Would this be said? Is this possible?":

> You create characters, which is a bit of a liberty anyway, then
> you give them words to speak and you give them a situation to
> play. And I find you've got to be very careful.

If the subtextual reality of each character has been imagined with fullness and accuracy, and if the actors have given a precise, solid and detailed actuality to it in their performance, then reader and audience may fitfully, progressively and perhaps, at last, with a kind of certainty, come to recognize it, each for themselves and in their own measure and time. The repetitions in the first episode of *The Birthday Party* can all be explained on slow analysis, but in performance the conflict between Petey and Meg is not put into irrevocable words at this stage of the play and therefore it is there only to be "sensed" by the audience. Pinter's plays are realistic in one important and unusual way: audience and readers do not know everything, and what certainty there is comes very late in the play. The plays offer an opportunity for understanding very like those fleeting and uncertain opportunities that are offered by life.

In effect, Pinter seems to play a game with his audience, giving only a few signposts on the way, a few landmarks or buoys to distinguish the hidden rock and sand. Like his characters, he seems to evade, to obscure intentionally, to blaze false trails. But his concentration on the truth of the dramatic fiction is such that we come to realize that he plays these games of necessity without setting out to do so. His view of his own characters and the situations in which they are placed makes his task a wary one. He plays hide-and-seek with his audience because he is deeply involved in this very game himself. This is how he sees and hears the world around him and within him.

When Pinter is fully engaged as dramatist, he is fully caught. He knows more than his audience and he knows the direction in which the play will go; but his involvement is to watch, wait and explore, and then to stretch out carefully in order to touch something which is not wholly expected, not wholly prepared for. The plays, written in this way, offer a sequence of partial discoveries, which the audience seem to make for themselves and out of which a sense of overall coherence and meaning seems to be born in each attentive consciousness. Pinter offers his own experience of discovery, and in the same mode of perception.

No detail of Pinter's writing can be adequately considered outside the context of the complete drama in which it must play its part. But by examining some short passages, his continuous control may be seen at work, and his awareness of the part words play in dramatic confrontations of considerable complexity but little explicit verbal statement. The more recurrent devices of language illustrate the nature of his perception and the means whereby he ensures that that perception is communicated in his writing.

The most difficult to describe is Pinter's manipulation of rhythms. Speeches run in one kind of phrasing, until some subtextual pressure lengthens, shortens or quickens the utterance and so, by sound alone, betrays the change of engagement. The last episode of *The Birthday Party* illustrates this:

> MEG *comes past the window and enters by the back door.* PETEY *studies the front page of the paper.*
> MEG *coming downstage*: The car's gone.
> PETEY: Yes.
> MEG: Have they gone?
> PETEY: Yes.

MEG: Won't they be in for lunch?

PETEY: No.

MEG: Oh, what a shame. *She puts her bag on the table.* It's hot
out. *She hangs her coat on a hook.* What are you doing?

PETEY: Reading.

MEG: Is it good?

PETEY: All right.

> *She sits by the table.*

MEG: Where's Stan?

> *Pause.*

Is Stan down yet, Petey?

PETEY: No . . . he's . . .

MEG: Is he still in bed?

PETEY: Yes, he's . . . still asleep.

MEG: Still? He'll be late for his breakfast.

PETEY: Let him . . . sleep.

> *Pause.*

MEG: Wasn't it a lovely party last night?

PETEY: I wasn't there.

MEG: Weren't you?

PETEY: I came in afterwards.

> *Pause.*

MEG: Oh. It was a lovely party. I haven't laughed so much for
years. We had dancing and singing. And games. You
should have been there.

PETEY: It was good, eh?

> *Pause.*

MEG: I was the belle of the ball.

PETEY: Were you?

MEG: Oh yes. They all said I was.

PETEY: I bet you were, too.

MEG: Oh, it's true. I was.

> *Pause.*

I know I was.

> *Curtain.*

Meg's first three speeches have two main stresses each, the third containing
a greater number of unstressed syllables; then, as she registers Petey's "No,"
the rhythm changes, starting with a single syllable "Oh," and then after a
comma three more, the middle one being unstressed: "Oh, what a shame."

She then moves about the room and begins speech again in much the same rhythms as at first. But when Petey replies this time, the phrasing grows shorter: "Is it good?" and then, having sat down, a simple two-stressed, two-syllabled "Where's Stan?" At this point there is a *Pause* during which her energy changes rhythm, for there now comes a slightly longer question, less emphatic, and "Petey" at the end following a comma's pause: "Is Stan down yet, Petey?" When Petey answers with broken phrasing and hesitation "No . . . he's . . . " she gains speed—"Is he still in bed?"—with light front vowels and no more than two stresses. But she then seems to halt with a monosyllabic question (that repeats "still" for the second time), but soon runs on with her observation, "He'll be late for his breakfast." This assumption of knowledge seems to allow her to change the whole mood of her thoughts, for a pause is now of her making; and when she speaks again, the rhythm is almost lilting, as if she were happily lost in idle thoughts: "Wasn't it a lovely party last night?" Petey's disclaimer breaks the mood momentarily, but after another pause, again of her own making, she picks up with a longer speech that has varied rhythms within it. The rhythmical jingle of ". . . dancing and singing" is followed by the shorter and slightly disturbing rhythm of a short, verbless sentence "And games"; this alludes to the frightening part of the evening. But then, as she remembers Petey was not there, the tension is again relaxed. Meg's final speeches begin again with a dreamy ease: "I was the belle of the ball"; but Petey's question and then his support tighten the rhythms. Her reply to the question starts with a two-syllable assertion, "Oh yes," and then a rather longer agreement, "They all said I was." Her reply to his token of support is short but with two pauses, the first slight and the second more emphatic: "Oh, it's true. I was." A *Pause* follows and then her last speech with two very short elements and a repeated "I" in its single phrase: "I know I was." The rhythm of this last utterance is short, contained and simple; and, since "know" carries more stress than "was," it has a slight falling-off. This tightening of the rhythm of speech is all the more effective for contrast with the lighter rhythms and longer reach of her preceding speeches.

Petey's rhythms start with stark monosyllables: "Yes . . . Yes . . . No." When Meg returns to the attack, they are less firm with two-syllables: "Reading . . . All right," the second giving an abrupt sound in comparison with the light ending of the first. When he is questioned about Stanley, his rhythms are broken, finding their firmest point on the concluding monosyllable, "sleep." Petey's next replies seem light, unstressed and smooth in comparison, as if yielding even as he contradicts Meg. When she enters her reverie, he seems to give light compliance with "It was good, eh?" and "I bet you were, too," each with a single syllable after a brief pause at the end of the line. The strongest contrast here is in the two-syllabled "Were you?" that could be delivered slowly or a little weighted.

The two characters have their own rhythms that are shown off by varied contrasts throughout the episode. But there is one point where they seem to speak almost in the same "breath," with a similar shortness of phrase, though with varying emphasis. This is when Petey's answers grow to "Reading" and "All right," and Meg shortens her questions to "Is it good?" and then "Where's Stan?" This rhythmic "meeting" may represent an unspoken acknowledgement of the one urgent matter they must both learn to face and live with. It lasts for only a moment that continues into the pause; then Meg's uncertainty forces the pace again.

If only the sounds of the words were heard, or if the dialogue was followed by someone not knowing a word of English, much of the pressures, tactics and moments of decision in this episode would be communicated. Such response might be more valid and exciting than if a reader registered the words without recreating their sound in his mind as well as registering their implications. Sound and the interplay of rhythms are constant factors in the effectiveness of Pinter's dialogue.

The same passage illustrates further devices of more occasional value. Most notable is barefaced, inescapable falsehood: the apparently simple statement of facts that the audience knows to be wrong. Here Petey fumbles towards his lie, but when it comes it is sharp enough to alert the audience: "Yes"—Stanley is still in bed. (The audience has just seen Petey watch Stanley march out of the room between Goldberg and McCann, despite his own protest.) The effect is not complete when Petey has given the simple lie, for so briefly it is effected that the elaboration which follows after another hesitation will also be listened to sharply for verification: "Yes, he's . . . still asleep." The audience now hears Petey as a man managing his wife and also his own unspoken thoughts. Meg's obvious lie—that "We had dancing" when, in fact, she had been unable to find a partner—is less crucially managed. It follows the more general deception of "It was a lovely party" and "They all said" she was "the belle of the ball." Here the comparatively small factual error is sufficient to alert attention and so give a momentary awareness of how far Meg is indulging her own fantasy of rosy success.

Falsehoods are important for Pinter's dialogue, not least when they can be detected only by careful reference from one scene to another—like Harry's pronouncement, in *The Collection*, that Stella's lamp is "beautiful." These provide clear clues for the actors, showing the nature of their varying commitment to speech and hence the varying pressure and tone of their utterance.

But even the most obscure falsehoods also serve to create a more general sense of suspicion in the audience, as each individual member catches, or thinks he catches, the character out.

Some of the more blatant lies are so casually delivered that the audience is encouraged to look for more than is going to be disclosed. This is a part of Pinter's two-pronged tactic of awakening the audience's desire for verification and repeatedly disappointing this desire. In *The Birthday Party* and *The Caretaker*, he may be said to create mystification by contrary statements and by the absence of verification for what can only be assumed. Where do the characters come from? (Answers are sometimes suggested, but never substantiated.) Is Goldberg's name Nat or Simey, or Benny? (Each name is used.) Was his son called Manney (Emanuel) or Timmy? (Again, each name is used.) Was Stanley married or not? (He is said to have a wife and also not to be married.) Why does Mick, in *The Caretaker*, invent such unlikely and impossible exploits for his uncle's brother who "married a Chinaman and went to Jamaica?" Why does Aston say Davies snores when on all but one, late, occasion he does not? The effect of such falsehoods, half-truths and contradictions is to raise suspicion about statements that could possibly be true, and which if true, might be significant. So the audience doubts and questions the characters' progress through the play, the clues they seem to drop, the assurance they seem to possess. Their words are undermined, their credit short.

A notable example is Aston's speech at the end of act 2 of *The Caretaker* which follows his strange stories about victimization. Here he tells of a mental hospital more in terms of primitive nightmare than medical practice. Yet there are details that could be true, like needing a guardian's permission for treatment and, more potentially reassuring for an audience, the credibility of its tone as a crazed man's account of actuality.

A fact which the audience has no cause to doubt is sometimes presented so that it awakens the possibility of relevance to some other statement of fact. For instance, is it significant that Stanley, in *The Birthday Party*, speaks of living in Basingstoke, when Goldberg has said his Uncle Barney had had a home just outside this town? Uncle Barney, the audience is told later, is the one whom Goldberg's father had said on his death-bed would always "see him in the clear." Coincidences like these tend to draw attention to each other. Why does Stanley say he connects McCann with a Fuller's teashop, a Boots Library and the High Street at Maidenhead, when, later in the same act, Goldberg, who did not hear this conversation, imagines his own life with some precisely similar detail: "Not size but quality. A little Austin, tea in Fullers, a library book from Boots, and I'm satisfied"? Has McCann reported back, or are Goldberg and Stanley connected in some previous activity? How does Goldberg know, or why does he say he knows, the date of Stanley's birthday? Or is that invention? Is there a connection between Goldberg talking of his surviving son (the other two sons were "lost—in an accident") and his pursuit of Stanley? (He says he "often" wonders what that son is doing now.) Or are McCann's two references to "the organization," while joining Goldberg in interrogating Stanley, a more reliable clue to the unknown past? Many of the accusations hurled at Stanley are absurd or impossible, so is any one of them "true"? Goldberg says, at length, that Stanley is being taken to Monty; but why does he merely hint that Monty is a doctor?

In a programme note for *The Caretaker*, Pinter claimed uncertainty as a key dramatic device:

> Given a man in a room, he will sooner or later receive a visitor. . .
>
> There is no guarantee, however, that he will possess a visiting card, with detailed information as to his last place of residence, last job, next job, number of dependents, etc. Nor, for the comfort of all, an identity card, nor a label on his chest. The desire for verification is understandable but cannot always be satisifed. There are no hard distinctions between what is real and what is unreal, nor between what is true and what is false. The thing is not necessarily either true or false; it can be both true and false. The assumption that to verify what has happened and what is happening presents few problems I take to be inaccurate. A character on the stage who can present no convincing argument or information as to his past experience, his present behaviour or his aspirations, nor give a comprehensive analysis of his motives is as legitimate and as worthy of attention as one who, alarmingly, can do all these things. The more acute the experience the less articulate its expression.

So presented, Pinter sounds as if he is making paradoxical play with words; and this is suitable. A more direct statement came in a letter to the *New York Times* in 1967, when *The Birthday Party* was presented on Broadway. A theatregoer had written to say that Mr. Pinter was shirking his job and should tell her who the two visitors were, where Stanley came from and whether they were "all supposed to be normal." Pinter replied that he couldn't understand her letter, and therefore couldn't reply until she had answered his questions: who was she, where did she come from and was she "supposed to be normal?" Pinter, in fact, is exploring Whitehead's dilemma, the inability of anyone to describe the fact that he exists and that he is attempting to communicate with others. The philosopher's questions yielded the dramatic device of blatant falsehood and continuous mystification and suspicion. Used with exaggeration and meticulous control, the device sharpens the audience's awareness of an uneasiness latent in all human encounters.

Of course, the lies Pinter introduces are not any lies. Often the clearest falsehoods introduce, or are accompanied by the most potent words, words which are found to reveal several levels of meaning or suggest a large wake of association. Petey's

> Yes, he's . . . still asleep.
> Let him . . . sleep.

says more than that Stanley, according to him, is in bed (which was the wording offered by Meg). As Petey had watched Stanley being escorted to the waiting black car, dressed in black, almost blind without his spectacles and quite silent, he could have seen him as if he were going to his own funeral. Moreover, the audience has witnessed Stanley reduced to child-like cries, and then drawing *a long breath which shudders down his body*. Just before Petey's entry he had crouched on a chair, shuddered, relaxed, dropped his head and become *still again, stooped*. After his "Birthday," Stanley has regressed as if into the womb, in a foetal position, but quiet and still as if dead. Is Stanley indeed being "put to sleep?" Or is Petey expressing his own fearful response in trying to let the sleeping lie? After this falsehood, Petey is, certainly, silent, as Stanley was and, probably, still is: is Petey "sleeping" too, intentionally?

Equally, Meg's "We had dancing and singing. And games. You should have been there," may be both, "true and false." Blind-man's-bluff was not the only "game" played; Lulu had had hers, Goldberg and McCann theirs; Stanley had been about to *strangle* her. Petey's absence at his "game" of chess had affected the course of the Birthday Party.

Pinter has an acute ear for those words which carry suggestions or traces of secondary implications. He places them carefully, often with a lie, as a stepping-off point for a long speech, or as a suddenly satisfactory conclusion to one, or as a conversation-stopper. They are often placed in unremarkable verbal surroundings, or seem to be uttered without reflection and then seized upon, as if a secret source of appropriateness has been unwittingly discovered.

JAMES EIGO

Pinter's Landscape

Harold Pinter's playwriting is frequently a triumph of noncommunication between his characters. Their dialogue abounds in contradictions, repetitions, delayed reactions, and small talk suggesting their reluctance or their inability to communicate. At moments of extreme tension, the dialogue can narrow to monologue. Pinter's first play, *The Room*, opens with a monologue that falls on deaf ears; in *The Caretaker* Aston's long speech establishes him as a sympathetic character. Not until *Landscape*, however, does Pinter limit all his dialogue to monologue.

At the most obvious level, this technique defines the separation of the play's characters, Beth and Duff. Duff often addresses Beth directly, but he never seems to hear her. And Beth seems totally unaware of Duff's presence. To summarise the plot is to list the contents of the separate monologues of Beth and Duff. Beth remembers a past love affair: a day at the beach with her unidentified lover and the subsequent drink at a hotel bar. The following day is spent alone, in the kitchen where we now find her. Her only utterances unrelated to these events are implicit contradictions. She wishes to go back to her former state, and yet she asserts that she is still beautiful.

Duff's monologue is not so confined. He remembers many incidents, and they are usually more recent than Beth's memories. Only the day before, he has visited a nearby park, where it rains, and the local pub, where he converses with a stranger. He also tells us that the dog disappeared the day before. His older memories provide some background for the couple's present

From *Modern Drama* 16, no. 2 (September 1973). © 1973 by the University of Toronto, Graduate Centre for the Study of Drama.

situation. Once servants employed by a Mr. Sykes, they now live alone in his country house. Duff remembers a trip with Mr. Sykes, a revelation to Beth that he has been unfaithful, their subsequent reconciliation, a visit to the pond with Beth, a dinner party with Syke's relatives, and his own violent attack on Beth. His memories are interspersed with pleas that Beth react to him, with expressions for hope in the future. Beth's memories are few and repetitive while Duff's repertory is more varied.

The monologues are puzzling in the theater because they seem so disparate. However, Pinter has related them subtly, above his characters' heads, as it were. Though the two characters talk at, rather than to, each other, their speeches interact at several points. Often these points of intersection emphasize the couple's isolation. Beth's account of her day spent lying near the ocean with her lover bears a superficial similarity to Duff's mention of a couple lying by the pond in the park. But Beth's account is romantic; the beach is an Eden. Duff's couple is forced to take shelter from the rain; his landscape offers nothing to balance the moisture, as the sand does in Beth's memory. Neither story of tenderness is relevant to the couple we see before us. One account belongs to the past while the other refers to strangers.

Many seemingly trivial details link the two monologues. Beth mentions "one exception" to the rule that men always treat her kindly; Duff provides the material for that exception in his recollection of tearing off the chain around Beth's waist. Beth alludes to her own gravity when arranging flowers, but when Duff concurs ("you didn't laugh much. You were . . . grave."), she counters with: "I laughed, with him." Duff mentions he would not feed ducks but sparrows; later he recalls that Beth fed the ducks. Both remember a blue dress that their employer gave to Beth. While Beth talks of the sea, Duff talks of fishing. Beth's account of the hotel bar intersects Duff's account of the pub; the former is elegant, the latter coarse. After Duff compliments Beth on her cooking, she remembers the lunch she cooked for her lover. Just as Beth and her lover are so close "they almost touch," Duff recalls: "Without touching you, I could feel your bottom." Furthermore, Duff remembers that on this occasion Beth looked out the window rather than at him. Beth can remember hearing her lover close behind her, but she does not look at him for she is busy arranging flowers. Duff fondly recalls how Beth would arrange flowers.

The couple's loneliness emerges from references to a dog. Duff's opening line is the announcement: "The dog's gone. I meant to tell you." The presence of the dog offered both characters an alternative to isolation. Duff took it to the park with him. Beth recalls sitting in the kitchen alone stroking the animal's head. The dog, now gone, can no longer offer any companionship.

One of the most suggestive and frequently repeated motifs is that of children. Early in the play Beth expresses the desire to mother the child of her lover. Duff tells how he took shelter with some children during a "downfall," but they soon ran away. The strange man with whom Duff converses in the pub remarks: "I haven't got a son. . . . I've never had any children." If we take Beth's remarks chronologically (as they occured in the past and not as they come back in memory), her last one is of children running below in the valley. These references are to children imagined, children hoped for, children far away, children that elude the couple's grasp. The suggestion of fruitless love is strong.

The frequency of intersecting themes suggests that though the characters do not actually hear each other, something filters through the barriers they have erected. These meeting points between the two monologues give the piece a subtle cohesion. Equally important is the use of similar details in conjunction with different incidents to suggest one of the major movements of the play: the merging of different times into one. Beth's present existence is totally confined to past memory. Duff's present differs from that of the woman in degree only, for his memories are not quite so old. But he is usually confined to the past. The points of intersection serve to show not only that the past blends with the present, but that there is more than one past, whose incidents merge. The final remembrances of both characters are repetitions of earlier recollections, but more and sometimes different details have accumulated. Thus, the validity of both memories, both pasts, is undermined. The similar details applied to both shared and isolated moments point to the existing ambiguity in the present relationship.

Though there are only two characters on stage, a series of triangles is mentioned or suggested. The angle of one triangle is Mr. Sykes, the other two angles formed by his servants, the couple on stage. He gives Beth a beautiful blue dress and many compliments. He accompanies Duff on a trip North and acknowledges his dependence on his male servant. Even though he has relatives (his mother and sister come to a mysterious dinner party), he leaves his house to the couple. Even so, Duff resents his former employer instead of being grateful to him. Duff calls him a "gloomy bugger' and remembers his nagging. After Syke's exit (death is not specifically mentioned), Beth continues to bang the gong as if he were still there. So immured is she in the past, that Duff can reclaim her only by assault, tearing from her the instruments by which she served her former master.

The second triangle was revealed to Beth almost immediately after Duff's trip with Sykes. It seems Duff had been unfaithful to her. He will go into no details as the girl is "unimportant." This focuses the attention not on the particular, but rather on the general act of infidelity. Beth forgives him, kissing his cradled face, just as she remembers kissing her lover's face.

The most imporant triangle is the one we can least certainly determine: that between Beth, her lover, and Duff. The lover's identity is not mentioned; the mystery creates a tension for the piece. Because of the strange relationship between the woman and her employer, there is a suggestion that it is he. But perhaps it is one who remains nameless. Since many of Beth's memories of her lover coincide with Duff's of his former relationship with Beth (e.g., a cradled kiss, nearness without touching), the man may be Duff himself. But if so, the lover can only be the man Duff was and no longer is, or a man he never was, a fabrication of Beth's imagination. The uncertainty of the third triangle is one of the many ambiguities that shroud the couple now dead to each other.

The present differences between the couple are carefully outlined and suggest possible reasons for the degeneration of their relationship. Beth remembers her man as gentle. They usually lie near each other, laughing softly. She will only drink tea. She arranges flowers and speaks in poetic terms. Duff remembers being gentle, but of late is only coarse. His drink is beer. In his speech vulgarities and obscenities occur frequently. He uses violent sexual terms to explain both the preparation of beer and his attack on Beth. He imagines raping her in the hallway, with the gong banging and the dog barking.

The physical landscape differs in the memories of the couple. Beth nearly merges with her landscape. She and her man are buried in the sand. Later, when she traces their figures in the sand, it slips so that their marred contours blend with the beach. She will never be able to escape her landscape, that of yesterday grafted on to the present and projected into the future. She becomes that landscape in the concluding moments of the play: "So sweetly the sand over me. . . . So silent the sky in my eyes. Gently the sound of the tide." Alliteration, assonance, and rhyme musicalise the blend.

Duff recalls the recent landscape. During a rainstorm Beth prefers looking out into the night to looking at him. The landscape becomes a metaphor for the couple's present situation. He knows only darkness, rain, excrement: "Mind you, there was lots of shit all over the place. Dogshit . . . duckshit . . . all kinds of shit . . . all over the paths. The rain didn't clean it up. It made it even more treacherous."

Perhaps the major difference between the two people is in what gives meaning to their lives. Duff is still so involved in Beth that he won't invite a few friends over for drinks: "It's not necessary." He later underlines this by saying that all that matters is that he and Beth are alone in the house.

But for Beth all meaning is past: "the lightness of your [the lover's] touch, the lightness of your look, my neck, your eyes; that is my meaning." But that meaning is trapped in another time, or never was. The lover and the employer are gone; her present companion is changed.

At no point in the play do the characters so diverge as they do in their final pronouncements. Language is a primary reason. Duff's one-syllable words and hard consonants beat out a staccato rhythm while Beth's longer words and liquid consonants flow melifluously. The language reflects the subject matter and underscores the couple's separation. Both speeches are visions of love, but the difference is striking. Duff tells of a rape; Beth, of lovemaking on her romantic landscape, the beach. The two visions of love exclude even as they complement each other. As long as this final difference exists, all hope for interaction is vain. Therefore, the technique of playlong monologues mirrors the emotional situation. Mr. Sykes once said that they made "a good team." Dramatically, if in no other way, this is true.

AUSTIN E. QUIGLEY

The Room

A common language is a sort of social switchboard which commands the power grid of the driving forces of the society. The meaning of a great deal of speech behaviour is just the combined personal and social forces it can mobilize and direct.
                                    —J. R. FIRTH, "The Tongues of Men"

Pinter's first play, *The Room*, is also one of his most puzzling works. Tension characterizes every relationship in the play though the sources of the tension are at best obliquely indicated. The conclusion focuses on the death of a blind Negro, who enters the play very late but is nonetheless central to the movement of the action portrayed. This late entry, with its consequent abridgement of information about the Negro, has inevitably led to a variety of inspired guesses about who he is and what he represents. As accuracy in this area is both essential and difficult we are confronted with considerable critical disagreement and a variety of interpretations.

The play is severally described as a failed satire, a "little allegory about life, death, and cosmic concepts," "about two people in a room and how they invest that room with the secrets of their concealed lives," "an existential drama," "an image of an aging woman's final confrontation with the reality of death," and "simply about people bothering people who want to keep to themselves." Hinchliffe extends the latter statement to a general comment on all of Pinter's plays, but as such it is inaccurate. Even as far as *The Room* is concerned, it glosses over a vital source of tension in the play: the tension between the desire to be left alone and the desire to know more about what one wants to be left alone by. This error is perpetuated by many critics and

From *The Pinter Problem*. © 1975 by Princeton University Press.

probably has its basis in Taylor's influential 1962 survey of modern English drama, *Anger and After*. His chapter on Pinter contains this comment on *The Room*'s main character: "essentially Rose, the Rose of the earlier scenes anyway, belongs to that group of characteristic Pinter figures from his first phase . . . those who simply fear the world outside." This generalization seems rather tenuous when applied to other plays and particularly misleading when applied to Rose. To miss the side of Rose's character that does more than "simply fear the world outside" is to miss the part of the play that prepares for the entry of the Negro. The latter is not only feared; he is also desired, and Rose is not the victim of an arbitrary intruder but the victim of her own fundamental ambivalence. Like the matchseller in *A Slight Ache* and Goldberg and McCann in *The Birthday Party*, the Negro bases his power as a disrupting intruder more on the individual vulnerabilities of Rose than on any remarkable powers of his own. This point is given physical emphasis in *A Slight Ache* and *The Room*, in which the intruders are silent and blind respectively, and it should be noted in both cases that the intruder is invited in. Rose is vulnerable because she is ambivalent about her role and her life in "the room" and this internal conflict is externalized in the final confrontation between Bert and Riley.

The basis of this ambivalence is of crucial importance to an understanding of the play, as the developments it gives rise to culminate in the arrival of Riley. The play is built around this gradual process, and in approaching its structure we need to recall Cohn's suggestion that Pinter's "dramatic building block continues to be the duologue which is a verbal duel." Applied with an awareness of the extensive scope that Pinter gives to the interrelational function of language, this suggestion provides us with an approach to the structure of the play. As indicated [elsewhere], relationships fuse the categories of theme and structure in a Pinter play, and it is the separate conversations, the duologues, in which developing relationships are explored, that provide the major units of development. *The Room* is made up of six such conversation-units. These conversations are linked by a series of recurring motifs, by the constant presence of Rose, and by the constant location—the room itself. They can be listed as follows:

1. Rose and Bert
2. Rose and Mr. Kidd (with Bert present)
3. Rose and Mr. and Mrs. Sands
4. Rose and Mr. Kidd (with Bert absent)
5. Rose and Riley
6. Rose, Riley, and Bert

We need to establish the significance of each of these units by describing their internal structure and also the external patterns that develop between them to form the unity of the play.

SECTION 1: ROSE AND BERT

Noting the constant tension in the relationships of Pinter's characters, Lois Gordon suggests that "Pinter's assault is levelled at the sources responsible for [the] terrible disparity between one's acts and impulses—civilization itself . . . the shackles and misery that are man's inevitable lot when he enters into the company of other men. . . . There is something about the nature of the individual that is incompatible with the communities of men." To generalize this problem to an assault on civilization is to move the point of focus from personal relationships toward ephemeral social structures of one kind or another. Pinter leads no assault on civilization or on anything else. His plays explore the more basic problem that Gordon mentions, the potential constraints imposed upon the individual when he comes into contact with other individuals. But these constraints are not wholly negative in nature; the constraints involved for a given person in a given relationship can also be balanced by compensations that the individual may find indispensable. As indicated [elsewhere], the central irony of Pinter's plays is that a character can only substantiate his sense of his individuality by operating in relationships which acknowledge and affirm that individuality; yet as soon as he enters into a relationship he is confronted with the complementary demands of his companion. The resulting compromise is negotiated in the dialogue, and if the conflicting demands are excessive the compromise can be one of dangerously balanced, rather than resolved, tensions.

It is the latter situation that we encounter in the opening scene of *The Room*. Rose talks, with Bert present, for an extended period, and Bert never enters into the potential conversation, even when addressed directly by name. As previously indicated, silence is not a neutral activity. By refusing to make the responses that would meet the demands of Rose's language, Bert is refusing to confirm that their relationship is as Rose would wish it to be. She casts him in the role of one dependent on her motherly supervision, and he simply refuses to participate in a conversation that defines their relationship in this way. But there is a second component to their relationship. Not only does Bert refuse to acknowledge Rose's demands, Rose also refuses to acknowledge Bert's silence. She continues to talk as if he were participating in her conversation on the terms she is dictating. There is no explicit acknowledgement of the friction between them. He never tells her to be quiet, and she never demands that he reply. We are faced with a relationship that has reached a fixed point of discord, a discord that is not acknowledged by either character but is manifest in every facet of their relationship.

The lack of explicit acknowledgement of their discord is important. If the discord were all that their relationship consisted of, they might just as well part. But, in fact, they stay together for reasons which are only gradually revealed, and this is a major function of the opening scene. Rose talks, partly to fill the silence, but mainly to record, reiterate, and reshape those components of her existence that give her life a meaning she can value. The room itself is one such component, and she dwells on its warmth, its cosiness, and its convenience: "If they ever ask you, Bert, I'm quite happy where I am. We're quiet, we're all right. You're happy up here. It's not far up either, when you come in from outside. And we're not bothered. And nobody bothers us." But the very fact of her saying this, the very need to verbalize what might well have been assumed, raises the possibility of her doubts as well as her reasons for overcoming those doubts. She is not simply trying to convince Bert, who probably isn't listening, anyway; she is also trying to convince herself. If this were only an isolated statement, it might simply indicate a savoring and sharing of satisfaction. But when it recurs several times, the strength of her inner doubt is increasingly confirmed by the persistent need to invalidate it.

> This is all right for me.
>
> . . . . this room's all right for me. I mean, you know where you are. When it's cold for instance.
>
> This is a good room. You've got a chance in a place like this. . . . Like when they offered us the basement here I said no straight off. I knew that'd be no good. The ceiling right on top of you. No, you've got a window here, you can move yourself, you can come home at night, if you have to go out, you can do your job, you can come home, you're all right. And I'm here. You stand a chance.

Rose's affirmation of the benefits of the room is contrasted with the room itself—a sparsely furnished place which serves Rose and Bert as bedroom, living room and kitchen combined. But for Rose it is a place which meets some of her needs. It gives her security and it gives her life a structure. In tending Bert's needs here she also ministers to her own.

Rose's attitude to the room is similar to her attitude to Bert. His shortcomings, like the room's, are dealt with by talking them out of existence.

Ignoring Bert's silence, she casts herself as one vitally concerned in providing Bert with food, information, advice, encouragement, nursing, and admiration. She constantly projects his needs in order to define for herself a variety of functions in their relationship. Whether her first priority is his needs or her own comes quickly into question as Bert's participation in her projections seems limited to consuming the food she cooks and serves. The information, the advice, the encouragement, and the admiration are all ignored, and Rose is left to fantasize the indispensable role she would have played if Bert had ever become seriously ill: "I'd have pulled you through." Here again the needs of her self-image seem to be served as much as any unselfish concern for Bert's health.

The most important aspect of the latter fantasy, however, is its link with her methods of reinforcing her valuation of the room. Rose constantly shores up her commitment to the life she leads by relying on comparisons with alternatives. Thus, the merits of the room are extolled by referring to the disadvantages of living in the basement or by contrasting the warmth and light inside with the dark and cold outside. The method itself is indicative of the paucity of obvious advantages displayed by the room. But more important, the range of comparison and the repetition of certain comparisons give us important information about Rose. It gradually becomes apparent that these comparisons are dwelt upon not only for the purpose of confirming the benefits of life in the room but also as a source of escape from the limitations of that life. To Rose, the room is not solely a haven, an escape from the outside—as many critics have suggested—though this is certainly one of its functions. In fact, she is also fascinated by and drawn toward the mysterious life that she has cut herself off from.

> *She rises, goes to the window, and looks out.*
> It's quiet. Be coming on for dark. There's no one about.
> *She stands, looking.*
> Wait a minute.
> *Pause.*
> I wonder who that is.
> *Pause.*
> No. I thought I saw someone.
> *Pause.*
> No.
> *She drops the curtain.*

Throughout this first scene Rose is uncertain about her commitment to the life she leads, and this uncertainty is repeatedly indicated in the detail

of her speech. On the one hand, she stresses the benefits of not being bothered
by people where they live, and, on the other, she is fascinated by the thought
of who might be living elsewhere in the house and who might be passing
outside. She emphasizes the benefit of the cosy warmth in the room but
dwells on the windy, cold world outside the house. But the most frequently
recurring manifestation of her ambivalence is her fascination with the basement of the house. While rejecting its value relative to their room, she returns
to it obsessively. Initially it seems merely an innocuous comparison:

> the room keeps warm. It's better than the basement, anyway.

But, as she returns repeatedly to this topic, it gradually takes on a greater
significance. The damp, running walls of the basement, its small size, its
low ceiling and lack of a window are all commented upon, but this repeated
emphasis on its unsuitability as a place to live is combined with speculations
as to who might nevertheless be living there.

> I wouldn't like to live in that basement. Did you ever see the
> walls? They were running.

> I don't know who lives down there now. Whoever it is, they're
> taking a big chance. Maybe they're foreigners.

> I wonder who has got it now. I've never seen them, or heard of
> them. But I think someone's down there.

Rose invests the basement with an ugliness and strangeness that goes well
beyond her need for advantageous comparison with her room. Even her
indication that it was once offered to them and that she, not Bert, turned it
down is insufficient justification for her obsession with it and its inhabitants.
Her compulsive dwelling on this topic subsequently gives rise to a comic
conversation between herself and Mr. Kidd, who fails to substantiate her
belief that it is so excessively uninhabitable.

> ROSE: It must get a bit damp downstairs.
> MR. KIDD: Not as bad as upstairs.
> ROSE: What about downstairs?
> MR. KIDD: Eh?
> ROSE: What about downstairs?
> MR. KIDD: What about it?
> ROSE: Must get a bit damp.
> MR. KIDD: A bit. Not as bad as upstairs though.
> ROSE: Why's that?

MR. KIDD: The rain comes in.
    Pause.

The short conversation runs at cross purposes as Mr. Kidd operates on the assumption that the topic is *dampness* in rooms, while for Rose the essential topic is the basement itself.

Mr. Kidd's straightforward attitude to the basement contrasts sharply with Rose's fascination with it, and this is important. Walter Kerr, commenting on the play, suggests that the room is a "solid-inside-a-void environment" in which "whatever impinges directly upon the consciousness is the sum total of what can be known." Outside the room is an alien unstructured void which can be commented on but cannot be defined or controlled. The mistake here is to accept Rose's version of the outside to the exclusion of the views of other characters. Mr. Kidd may be evasive at times, but he talks as if the world outside is fully structured. The Sands mention the quiet district the house is located in and comment on the pleasant appearance of its exterior. Bert, too, seems to have no trouble locating and driving his van, and overall there is enough to suggest that the world outside is quite a normal one. What Kerr has done is to accept as valid an image of the world outside which is in fact a projection of Rose's inner needs. The cold, dark, damp, windy, alien world that Rose describes tells us more about Rose than about the world outside. She is fascinated by what she describes as repulsive. The unpleasantness of her view of the world outside is born of her need to believe it is ugly in order to substantiate her contentment at being inside. But even in its ugliness, the outer world obsesses her, and her internal tension is externalized in the back and forth motion of the rocking chair to which she repeatedly returns.

Lacking the verbal confirmation she needs from Bert, Rose uses repetition and contrast to keep herself content in Bert's world. But the contrasts themselves become fascinating because they *are* other possibilities, not just because they show her present state in a beneficent light. Bert's refusal to serve as a mode of confirmation of Rose's role in life turns her elsewhere for a substitute, and this substitute, this method of advantageous comparison, begins gradually to reveal the possiblilty of a life in which Bert is totally substituted. The preparation for Riley's entry and the foundation of his power develop directly from the internal conflict that Rose demonstrates in this opening scene. Far from being a *deus ex machina*, Riley focuses and externalizes a side of Rose's character which, though severely restricted at the beginning of the play, is nonetheless manifest in her opening meandering speech. But while the opening scene provides clear, if often missed, indications of the significance of the play's conclusion, it does not provide much indication of what gave rise to the opening situation. For that we must go on to other sections.

SECTION 2: ROSE AND MR. KIDD—BERT PRESENT

With Mr. Kidd's entry, we have someone available who is ready and willing to converse with Rose. The latter's one-sided, complex speech to her silent husband gives way to what promises to be a more "normal" form of conversation. But instead of becoming more clear, the problems and ambiguities of the opening section are multiplied by the landlord's readiness to converse. The volubility of Kidd, like the silence of Bert, serves only to increase the uncertainties of Rose's world. Language, like silence, can be a means of evasion. But it would be wrong to follow Hinchliffe and conclude that Mr. Kidd "arrives, talks, but does not communicate." To suggest that "His conversation tells Rose nothing" is to fall into the error of believing that language carries information in only one way. In fact, his conversation tells Rose enough to make her very suspicious of his honesty. His regular failure to meet the terms of Rose's questions has prompted many critics to regard him as deaf, senile, or insane. But as Esslin points out, he "displays no symptoms of mental incapacity" elsewhere in the play, and his hearing seems unexceptionable later when he is persuading Rose to admit Riley.

Once we reject these explanations of his conduct, we are on the way to realizing that in the world of the play the odd opening "conversation" between Rose and Bert is not really so very odd. It is merely one example of what is also true of the Rose/Kidd relationship and of all the relationships in the play. Language is not used in these relationships simply to convey objective information. Rather, it is an instrument open to a variety of uses in the *process* of relating to others. Mr. Kidd's oblique response to Rose's language is not a sign of insanity; it is a mode of refusal, a method of evasion. Like Bert, he is not ready to tell Rose all she wants to know; he is not willing to allow her to relate to him as one who is entitled to know the details of his life. The details themselves may be trivial, but if Rose, or anyone else, wants to know them, then they may have a significance that has hitherto eluded him. His language, like Bert's silence, is a defense against forces that he feels are antagonistic. Pinter's comment on the "failure of communication" issue is useful here: "I believe the contrary. I think that we communciate only too well . . . and that what takes place is continual evasion, desperate rearguard attempts to keep ourselves to ourselves. Communcation is too alarming. To enter into someone else's life is too frightening. To disclose to others the poverty within us is too fearsome a possibility." It is this, not senility, that prompts Kidd to reply to Rose in the following manner:

ROSE: How many floors you got in this house?
MR. KIDD: Floors. *(He laughs.)* Ah, we had a good few of them in the old days.
ROSE: How many have you got now?
MR. KIDD: Well, to tell you the truth, I don't count them now.

Likewise, it is overconcern for his social image as landlord of a good house, rather than hearing problems, that accounts for his excessive denial of Rose's suggestion that he had a female help in the house.

ROSE: I thought you had a woman to help.
MR. KIDD: I haven't got any woman.
ROSE: I thought you had one when we first came.
MR. KIDD: No women here.
ROSE: Maybe I was thinking of somewhere else.
MR. KIDD: Plenty of women round the corner. Not here though.
       Oh no. Eh, have I seen that before?

Reacting to what he feels are the implications of Rose's remarks, Kidd interprets her suggestions as an attack on his moral status and he defends himself first by denial and then by changing the subject to counterattack Rose. His final sentence above leads into an assertion of previous knowledge of her room. To Rose, whose life is so intimately bound up with the room, this is indeed a vulnerable area. Kidd hints that the rocking chair has a hidden significance, which might seem trivial out of context, but in terms of their conflict is a subtle move.

The conversation between the pair becomes a series of attacks, evasions, and counterattacks as each seeks to outmaneuver the other, and Kidd's defensive maneuvering gives further indication of the diversity of language dominated by the interrelational function. As was suggested [elsewhere], there is a continuum of possible responses to a given statement, running from silence at one end to total conformity on the other. But within the continuum are a vast number of ways of responding in terms of the former pole with answers disguised as ones from the latter pole; Kidd makes full use of these as he gets into awkward situations:

ROSE: When did she die then, your sister?
MR. KIDD: Yes, that's right, it was after she died that I must have stopped counting.

Here the topic of the death of the sister is responded to, but not the essence of the question, which dealt with time. The utterances are linked, but obliquely.

> ROSE: When was this your bedroom?
> MR. KIDD: A good while back.

Kidd's response this time meets the request for a time specification but supplies only a vague time instead of the precision Rose seeks.

The battle continues with Rose questioning his hearing her husband drive off in the morning on the grounds that his bedroom is at the back of the house and out of earshot. He evades this by refusing to confirm the whereabouts of his bedroom and by saying that he was somewhere else at the time—again not specifying where. Kidd then counterattacks by reminding Rose of her status as tenant and temporary occupant of the room she so depends on: "This was my bedroom. . . . when I lived here," he remarks, and indicates Rose's beloved room. This, in terms of the battle, is a lethal remark, and Kidd, far from being senile, seems very perceptive in pinpointing Rose's vulnerabilities. The conversation becomes a battle over who can claim or suggest knowledge of the other's life in a threatening area. Pinter indicates beautifully the maneuvering mind of Rose when she returns some two pages later to the bedroom topic, using it as a means of catching Kidd off guard. The question derives from her earlier query of how he could hear her husband leaving in the morning, but she manages to present it in matter-of-fact terms as a restart to conversation after a pause. The apparently innocent question is anything but innocent: "Where's your bedroom now then, Mr. Kidd?" Pinning down the whereabouts of his bedroom has become a focus of their conflict, and he is well tuned-in to the nature of the attack: "Me? I can take my pick." This is a neat evasion, but unfortunately contradicts his statement five lines earlier that the house is "packed out."

It is examples like the latter that led Taylor to believe that Pinter was engaging in cheap mystification by matching statements of fact with statements of the contrary: "The technique of casting doubt upon everything by matching each apparently clear and unequivocal statement with an equally clear and unequivocal statement of its contrary . . . is one which we shall find used constantly in Pinter's plays to create an air of mystery and uncertainty." As was pointed out [elsewhere], this is not the technique, and this is not the purpose. The contradictions are not born of a simple desire to confuse the audience. Rather, they occur because the truth or falsity of a statement is not a dominant criterion for its use. The appeal of "facts" is subordinated to and governed by the interrelational requirement of the situation at hand. In this situation it is not "truth" that gives a set of statements its power, but consistency. A character's strength is a function of his capacity to uphold consistent positions in the face of a variety of conflicting demands; and, conversely, the major failure for a participant is inconsistency. Thus Kidd is being outmaneuvered by Rose when he contradicts himself on how full his house is, and this, not mystification, is the point of the contrast. As Kidd becomes increasingly flustered by Rose's persistent questioning, we perceive an oblique indication of one of the causes of Bert's silence. Her attempt to disorient and dominate Mr. Kidd parallels her excessive mothering of Bert in the opening section. Her concern over what Bert does and what he wears, and her readiness even to pour the salt and pepper on his meal for him begin to look like symptoms of a constant urge to dominate the men in her life. Her ability to outtalk Mr. Kidd hints at a possible earlier stage of her relationship with Bert.

Defending himself against further questioning on the organization of his house, Mr. Kidd goes off on a reminiscence about his sister and his family. But unlike Rose, Mr. Kidd's control of his language is not commensurate with the demands he makes on it. Unnerved by Rose's questioning, he gets himself into a series of difficulties. He becomes confused over whether his mother was a Jewess, whether his sister or mother had many children, and what his sister died of. An important indicator of the doubtful veracity of his statements and his loss of control of the situation is his misuse of two words. He refers to his mother's offspring as "babies" (when they would be much more likely to come to mind as his brothers and sisters), and he refers to his sister's bedroom as her "boudoir" (an indication of a possible confusion of memories of a sister with memories or fantasies of a different female relationship). It is partly this misuse of words that prompts Rose to exclaim on his exit "I don't believe he had a sister, ever." The inappropriate use of words is as revealing as the inconsistent assertion of facts. Both reveal Mr. Kidd's inability to cope with Rose in the process of verbal interaction. In Kidd's talking to Rose we find an indication of why Bert maintains a silence. To resist Rose's domineering, Mr. Kidd talks. To resist Rose's domineering, Bert remains silent. Both methods are partially effective, but both demand their price.

SECTION 3: ROSE AND MR. AND MRS. SANDS

The Rose/Kidd section served us with one pole of comparison for the relationship between Rose and Bert; the Sands's relationship provides us with another. At first glance, the marriage of this voluble couple seems to contrast strongly with the marriage of Rose and Bert with its rather different version of oblique conversation. Before we look further at the Sands's relationship, however, we must note one very important point. Though Rose is initially shocked by the discovery of the Sands just outside her door, she reveals few qualms about inviting them in. This supports the point that she is not just clinging to her room as a haven and escape from the outside. She is constantly struggling to reconcile her fears and insecurities to the persistent curiosity that she feels toward people outside the room. The invitation to the Sands links with her preoccupation with people outside, people in the basement, Mr. Kidd's activities, etc., to underline her interest in what lies beyond the room.

Unlike the preceding relationships introduced in the play, the Rose/Sands relationship seems to have no previous history. Their meeting seems simply to be the product of the chance opening of a door. And once they leave we never hear from them again. But their entry at this point does more than simply provide another married couple with whom we can compare Rose and Bert. It also provides us with an indication of how Rose copes with strangers. The Rose/Sands relationship needs structuring from the foundations up. Much of their opening dialogue is therefore filled with questions and a tentative search for common ground. It is important to grasp the contrast of this uncertain conversation with Rose's much more positive attitude toward Riley when he enters later.

Confusion is an immediate factor in the embryonic relationship of Rose and the Sands. But the focus of that confusion is an issue that Rose finds rather disturbing. The Sands's assertion that the landlord is not called Kidd threatens to undermine the organization and security of Rose's world, for it is he who gives her authority over her room. But, in spite of her vulnerability in this area, she betrays no qualms about inviting the Sands to come in. And once inside, their marital disharmony provides an indication of their function in the play.

The immediate battle between Mr. and Mrs. Sands over whether he should sit down or not characterizes the stage of their marital relationship. Unlike Rose and Bert, who have reached a fixed point of maladjustment, the Sands are constantly in the process of establishing their relationship. Each tries to dominate the other, and each attempts to achieve this by outtalking the other. They argue over whether he needs to sit down, over whether or not Mrs. Sands saw a star, over the length of time they have been in the building, and over the usage of "perch" and "sit." Always there are two opposed versions and no agreed source of authoritative settlement. When Mrs. Sands challenges Mr. Sands's denial that she saw a star and demands proof, he provides a significant response:

MR. SANDS: You didn't see a star.

MRS. SANDS: Why not?

MR. SANDS: Because I'm telling you. I'm telling you you didn't
see a star.

Acceptable facts in the Pinter world are, as we have stated, those that small groups commonly agree to be true. When disagreement occurs and only two people are involved, validity is established by the dominant partner, as we saw with Gus and Ben. As "validity" and "reality" dictate relationships and relationships define the individual, the conflicts in this area can be extreme—as they are here in the Sands's relationship. The particular topic is secondary, but the issue is always crucial and, in a nonphysical sense, violent. Mr. Sands invokes a single standard for truth—his language; it is so because he *says* so: "Because I'm telling you. I'm telling you you didn't see a star." In the light of the wearying conflict of the Sands, the Rose/Bert relationship takes on a clarifying perspective as a later stage in the same battle. The seeds of Rose's internal ambivalence are present in the conflict that Mrs. Sands faces over her urge to dominate her husband and his complementary efforts to dominate her. As long as she is unsuccessful she faces constant battling and constant instability. But if she succeeds, a possible result is a more stable, but equally unsatisfactory, passive resistance of the kind we see in Bert. In this depiction of two unsatisfactory marital relationships, Pinter prepares the way for another choice, embodied in the entry of Riley.

The scene with the Sands has another important function. Rose's domineering of her male companions has been shown in her relationships with Bert and Mr. Kidd and paralleled by Mrs. Sands's attacks on Mr. Sands. But we see Rose in another light when Mr. Sands seeks to establish control over her. Torn between curiosity and fear, she becomes evasive when asked direct questions that put her world up for external corroboration, but after she learns that the Sands have visited the basement her curiosity impels her to pursue the conversation. Unnerved at first by Mr. Sands's demands for knowledge about the whereabouts of the landlord, she begins to build the verbal barriers that she feels will protect her. The parallel with the behavior of Mr. Kidd in the previous scene is unmistakable as she becomes evasive and subordinates the validity of "facts" to their usefulness in defending her current situation. She denies even knowing Mr. Kidd and reinforces her position with: "We're very quiet. We keep ourselves to ourselves. I never interfere. I mean, why should I? We've got our room. We don't bother anyone else. That's the way it should be." But the other side of Rose's character soon reasserts itself. In spite of the fears that generated this insistence on her ignorance of and lack of interest in anything outside the room, her obsessive fascination with the basement soon proves stronger. Less than ten lines later she switches from defensive withdrawal to persistent questioning as the inherent dichotomy in her character manifests itself once more. Mrs. Sands's mention of a man in the basement grips her attention: "A man? . . . One man? . . . You say you saw a man downstairs, in the basement?" She is so obsessed by this that she is not even distracted by the vicious argument that occurs between the Sands at this point. But she is distracted when Mrs. Sands triggers her fears once more by contradicting herself. Rose's hypersensitivity to possible danger homes in on Mrs. Sands's statement that they were on their way *down* stairs when Mrs. Hudd opened the door on them.

> ROSE: You said you were going up.
> MRS. SANDS: What?
> ROSE: You said you were going up before.
> MRS. SANDS: No, we were coming down.
> ROSE: You didn't say that before.

But the strength of her fascination with the basement overcomes these suspicions very quickly. Rose's internal conflict is clearly indicated by these rapid switches from fear and withdrawal to curiosity and a demand to know.

> ROSE: This man, what was he like, was he old?
> MRS. SANDS: We didn't see him.
> ROSE: Was he old?
>   *Pause.*

At this point in the play, many threads of development converge on the basement. Apparently random details begin to form a pattern with its central focus pointing to this mysterious room. What began in section 1 as an innocuous comparison, "the room keeps warm. It's better than the basement, anyway," has gradually developed into something potentially much greater. The piece by piece indication of its characteristics has made it into a microcosm of Rose's version of the external macrocosm. Her fearful hints of the nature of what lies outside her room have repeatedly invoked a cold, damp, dark, inhospitable world, peopled with strangers, and the basement has become something of an archetypal example. And on this particualr evening, Rose's estimate of the world outside her room receives partial confirmation in the Sands's report on their experiences since entering the house.

> ROSE: What's it like out?
> MRS. SANDS: It's very dark out.

MR. SANDS: No darker than in.

MRS. SANDS: He's right there.

MR. SANDS: It's darker in than out, for my money.

MRS. SANDS: There's not much light in this place, is there, Mrs.
    Hudd? Do you know, this is the first bit of light we've
    seen since we came in?

This confirmation of the contrast between the room and the world outside
is only the first of Rose's projections that the Sands lend support to; the next
is Rose's image of the basement:

MRS. SANDS: I felt a bit of damp when we were in the basement
    just now. . . .

ROSE: What was it like down there?

MR. SANDS: Couldn't see a thing.

ROSE: Why not?

MR. SANDS: There wasn't any light.

The darkness and dampness of the basement are stressed again as Mrs. Sands
gives Rose a longer account of their movements in the building, and she goes
on to confirm yet another of Rose's fantasies—the presence of someone rather
strange in the basement:

it was very dark in the hall and there wasn't anyone about. So
we went down to the basement. Well, we got down there only
due to Toddy having such good eyesight really. Between you
and me, I didn't like the look of it much, I mean the feel, we
couldn't make much out, it smelt damp to me. . . . we couldn't
see where we were going, well, it seemed to me it got darker the
more we went, the further we went in . . . then this voice said,
this voice came—it said—well, it gave me a bit of a fright . . .
this man, this voice really, I think he was behind the partition,
said yes there was a room vacant. He was very polite, I thought,
but we never saw him, I don't know why they never put a light
on.

The still circumstantial link between the characteristics of the basement on
this particular evening and Rose's projection of a dark, damp, alien world
is made concrete by Mr. Sands's startling addition to his wife's account. As
Rose, unnerved by these reports of her fears/hopes coming true, tries to get
rid of the Sands by denying that there are any rooms for rent, Mr. Sands
counters:

MR. SANDS: The man in the basement said there was one. One
　　room. Number seven he said.
　　Pause.
ROSE: That's this room. . . . This room is occupied.

At this point the Sands leave, but their unexpected corroboration of
Rose's vision of the basement, together with the confirmation of a link between the inhabitant of the basement and the room that Rose lives in, has
developed what seemed only to be Rose's fantasies to a point at which fantasy
has a potentially concrete link with reality.

MR. SANDS: Haven't you ever been down there, Mrs. Hudd?
ROSE: On yes, once, a long time ago.
MR. SANDS: Well, you know what it's like then, don't you?
ROSE: It was a long time ago.

SECTION 4: ROSE AND MR. KIDD

The section opens with a conversation at comic cross-purposes which
makes the ironic point that confusion can arise as easily between two people
bent on communicating directly to each other as between two people who
are being mutually evasive. But the sources of this confusion reveal a further
irony; the conflict over which of two urgent topics should be discussed by
the two characters effectively externalizes the confusion within Rose. The
topic she wants to discuss (the security of her room-rental) and the topic
Mr. Kidd wants to discuss (the stranger in the basement) manifest the conflicting concerns of Rose's inner self. Her private conflict has become and
continues to become increasingly public as the play progresses and the route
to the entry of Riley is clearly charted.

Rose's oscillations between fear and curiosity become increasingly pain-
ful for her as the issues that hinge upon them become increasingly concrete.
In the midst of frantic questioning of Mr. Kidd about the security of her
room-rental, she is stopped abruptly by his shattering demand:

MR. KIDD: You'll have to see him. I can't take it any more.
　　You've got to see him.
　　Pause.
ROSE: Who?
MR. KIDD: The man. He's been waiting to see you. He wants to
　　see you. I can't get rid of him. . . . You've got to see him.

Significantly, the unnamed man will not come and simply break in on Rose;
he insists on waiting until he is invited.

MR. KIDD: I said, you can go up, go up, have done with it. No,
he says, you must ask her if she'll see me. . . . He just lies
there, that's all, waiting.

Also, it is Rose, not Mr. Kidd, who locates the place where the unnamed
visitor is waiting:

ROSE: He lies there, in the basement?

Rose's internal conflict, previously manifest in dual-purpose projections
of alternatives to her current life, now actualizes itself in the choice of whether
or not to see the unknown stranger in the basement. Who the stranger might
be is not as important as what his possible presence means to her. Fantasized
alternatives to her current life do not put it at imminent risk. But to confront
in person a representative of her inner needs requires a choice that might
prove irrevocable. The timid, feaful side of Rose's nature recoils from the
prospect:

ROSE: See him? I beg your pardon, Mr. Kidd. I don't know
him. Why should I see him?
MR. KIDD: You won't see him?
ROSE: Do you expect me to see someone I don't know? With
my husband not here too?
MR. KIDD: But he knows you, Mrs. Hudd, he knows you.
ROSE: How could he, Mr. Kidd, when I don't know him?
MR. KIDD: You must know him.
ROSE: But I don't know anybody. We're quiet here. We've just
moved into the district.

Once more, the tactic of the insecure, excessive denial, comes to the fore as
Rose casts herself in the role of a loyal wife totally dependent on her husband
and his interests. Her strident, "Do you expect me to see someone I don't
know? With my husband not here too?" asserts a self-image of loyalty to
Bert and conformity to the nicest social rules. But within seconds, the image
is undercut by a greater fear that the man might visit her, not when Bert is
absent, but when he is present. If Rose were, in fact, the simple, loyal wife
whose image she invokes, then this possiblity would not worry her. It is
this ambivalence, this fundamental dichotomy in her character, that makes
her vulnerable in this stituation. It is this that forms the basis of the newcomer's power. Rose is not simply the victim of Bert, or of Riley; rather,
the play brings to a head the inherent instability of her opening situation.
What was at best an uneasy compromise now becomes the operative factor

in a critical dilemma. If she invites the man in, she runs the risk of having Bert return and discover them. If she refuses to invite him, she runs the risk of having him call when Bert is present. That both situations seem threatening to her is a function of her inner betrayal of Bert and the possibility that this betrayal might become evident in the presence of the visitor.

Precisely why the visitor should be repugnant to Bert is not made clear at this point and is never finally clarified. Ultimately, it is not of central importance. The precise nature of Rose's betrayal of Bert is not pinned down to the morality or validity of any particular event in her past because this is not the locus of the play's concerns. Rose's vulnerability to the threat of betrayal is more significant than what the particular betrayal might be. This vulnerability is sufficient proof of her disloyalty to Bert, and it registers in her behavior even before the newcomer is named. The man downstairs is not identified when Mr. Kidd reports that he prefers to wait for Bert to leave before confronting Rose. He is likewise unidentified when Rose recoils in fear at Mr. Kidd's threat:

> MR. KIDD: I know what he'll do. I know what he'll do. If you
> don't see him now, there'll be nothing else for it, he'll
> come up on his own bat, when your husband's here, that's
> what he'll do. He'll come up when Mr. Hudd's here,
> when your husband's here.
> ROSE: He'd never do that. . . . He wouldn't do that.
> MR. KIDD: Oh yes. I know it.

Mr. Kidd, in fact, is merely using this potential threat to get the visitor off his hands and out of his way. His only grounds for believing that this would be a threat to Rose is her readiness to react to it as such. Her control of her own life is beginning to slip from her hands as the power of the repressed side of her character makes itself felt. Her subsequent confrontation with the visitor takes on the form of a decisive battle between the timid, withdrawn side of her nature and the curious, outgoing side that urges her to align herself with a life very different from the one she lives with Bert:

> Fetch him. Quick. Quick!

SECTION 5: ROSE AND RILEY

The entry of the man from the basement is, of course, a fine theatrical moment. His arrival brings to a crisis the conflict between the two sides of Rose's ambivalent character, and his presence becomes the focal point of both her fear and her curiosity. On the one hand, he confirms her fear of coldness, darkness, and otherness in the world outside, and, on the other, he justifies her obsessive curiosity about the possibility of an unknown and perhaps foreign presence in the mysterious basement. That he should be black and blind strikes one as both surprising and appropriate. Rose's behavior strikes us the same way. The role she adopts relative to him is unlike anything she has revealed so far, yet given the thoroughgoing ambivalence of her nature, the "new" Rose seems a recognizable mutation.

When we recall the sparring and questioning that characterized Rose's first meeting with the Sands, we see by contrast an important aspect of Rose's attitude to the newcomer. She immediately assumes a crude aggressiveness and authority, as if she has categorized him in advance. She questions not only his mission but his right to have any mission involving her. The extremity of her behavior serves only to undermine its credibility. Calling him a "creep" and a "cripple," she struggles to define the relationship on terms that give her control. Riley is not as easily outmaneuvered, however, and refuses to answer demands put to him in those terms. This refusal undermines Rose's attempts to control the situation, and as she strains ever harder to impose her authoirty on him she is forced to resort to shoring up her vision of herself: "I can keep up with you. I'm one ahead of people like you. Tell me what you want and get out." This explicit verbalizing of attitude and intent is more like the relationship of Mr. and Mrs. Sands than anything Rose has revealed in her conversations with Bert and Mr. Kidd. In contrast, the visitor is quiet and self-controlled, saying simply, "My name is Riley." The calmness of this response serves only to make Rose's attitude even more extreme as she waxes vitriolic about Riley and his peers. These insults, however, have no visible impact on Riley, who simply announces in measured tones: "I want to see you" and then lapses into silence. Riley's imperturbability is an obvious manifestation of resistance to Rose's influence, and she switches back and forth between different methods of gaining control over the situation. On the one hand, she stresses his weaknesses: "Well you can't see me, can you? You're a blind man. An old, poor blind man. Aren't you? Can't see a dickeybird." On the other, she denies any knowledge of him, claiming to be insulted at the possibility. Yet in the face of his silence she continues to attempt to clarify his relationship to her. She pictures him as a customer, as a beggar, and as a source of scandal, but none of these strikes any chord in Riley.

Eventually, Rose reverts to the aggressive demand that he tell her what he wants, and Riley's response brings her ambivalent character to another state of crisis. When he replies, "I have a message for you," he triggers once

more the conflict between fear and curiosity that makes Rose's life so unstable. But this time the resolution is crucial. Her first reaction is to scoff
at the possibility of his having a message—"How could you have a message
for me, Mister Riley, when I don't know you and nobody knows I'm here
and I don't know anybody anyway?"—and she goes on to insult him again.
This attitude, the side of Rose born of her fears and insecurities, the side
that attaches her firmly to the silent Bert, elicits no response from the inscrutable Riley. There is a pause, and in that pause the balance of Rose's
world shifts irrevocably. The other side of her character emerges, questioning
and curious:

What message? Who have you got a message from? Who?

To this side of her character, Riley responds immediately: "Your father
wants you to come home." The part of Rose that needs to look outward,
afraid, but mainly curious, finally gains dominance over the part that is
mainly afraid and needs the room and needs Bert. The latter side of her
character, which insulted Riley and refused to acknowledge him, temporarily
disappears. With the change comes a change of name. Riley, who initially
addressed her as Mrs. Hudd, now calls her Sal and calls her home. The
room, always defined in contrast to other things, now falls in contrast to
"home." It loses its haven characteristics and becomes only "here." With the
loss of those characteristics goes the life which Rose has tried to build verbally
upon it. That life is seen anew as repugnant:

ROSE: I've been here.
RILEY: Yes.
ROSE: Long.
RILEY: Yes.
ROSE: The day is a hump. I never go out.
RILEY: No.
ROSE: I've been here.
RILEY: Come home now, Sal.

We have here the verbal reinforcement of a shared reality that Bert has long
denied Rose. Riley's monosyllabic responses are crucial statements for Rose,
who finds in this relationship the common ground of "reality" which her
previous life in the room significantly lacked. The virtues of that life crumble
as one verbal illusion is substituted for another. Staying within the room is
now pictured as repugnant: "The day is a hump. I never go out." Stroking
the Negro's head, she recognizes a self that has been long repressed in the
relationship with Bert. But peace is not to be found here. The side of Rose

that longs for the room and its security is, at this point, transcended in the relationship with Riley, but its strength is by no means extinguished.

SECTION 6: ROSE, RILEY, AND BERT

The unacknowledged gulf between Rose and Bert has surfaced in Rose in the scene with Riley. In this section its presence can no longer be denied between Rose and Bert, and this new explicitness in their relationship alters it irrevocably. Darkness, associated with Rose's suppressed life, with her curiosity, and with the world outside, has entered the room in the shape of the Negro. When Bert draws the curtain of the room as he enters, he is no longer separating two forms of reality; the curtain has become a mere arbitrary line in a black continuum. The Sands regarded Rose's room as the only area of light in a darkened building; now the stage direction says explicitly that within the room "It is dark." Rose, ever ambivalent and afraid, goes toward Bert as he enters and responds uneasily to his opening remarks. But Bert's references to his journey, his first remarks in the play, significantly transfer to his van the concern for femininity that he has never revealed for Rose. His domineering references to the van parallel Rose's earlier domineering attitude toward him. Their incompatible urges to dominate are made clear in this speech, as is also Bert's parallel attempt to find outside their maladjusted relationship a means of manifesting that which compromise had repressed within it. Rose responds to his mention of the dark and cold of his journey but recoils into silence at the insistent stress on his power over the "female" van:

> BERT: I drove her down, hard. They got it dark out.
> ROSE: Yes.
> BERT: Then I drove her back, hard. They got it very icy out.
> ROSE: Yes.
> BERT: But I drove her.
> *Pause.*
> I sped her.
> I caned her along.

It is now Bert, not Rose, who is creating a verbal world that conforms to his needs, and it is now Rose, not Bert, who is required to give confirmation of this world. But Rose, like Bert earlier, lapses instead into silence. Bert's loss of Rose becomes manifest in the dialogue as she ceases to provide verbal reinforcement to his statements. Like Rose at the beginning of the play, he is forced to repeat and rephrase himself, to supply his own confirmation of the nature of his world. As Rose's responses cease, he is left to face the isolation of his needs.

With realization dawning on him, he lashes out at the only available focus of their new disharmony and beats Riley to death. But the change in Rose is irrevocable, and their old relationship no longer viable. Rose stands and clutches her eyes:

> Can't see. I can't see. I can't see.
> *Blackout.*
> *Curtain.*

The stage is plunged into darkness as Rose's final cry confirms the priority of her link with the Negro over that with Bert. This is its major significance. It is not naturalistic, but it completes the pattern. The internal conflict between two sides of Rose's character is finally externalized in this clash between Riley and Bert. No victory is possible between them because no solution is possible. The loss of whatever possibilities the Negro represented for Rose leaves part of her mutilated. But to lose Bert would equally rob her of a strength necessary to her security, a strength Riley conspicuously lacks.

Much ink has been spilled in trying to account for Riley and for Rose's and Bert's reactions to him in terms of hypothetical resconstructions of Rose's past. As the play gives us no more than a hint of this, it is obviously an unnecessary quest. To regard the Negro as a symbol of death, fate, age, or whatever is also to go beyond the demands of the play. The play operates in the realm of variable character, uncertain fact, and unspecified fears. To label any of these is to change the play. We only have the parameters of performance to guide us, and these parameters specify things only up to a certain point and no further. The blackness of Riley and Rose's blindness symbolize only the connection between them. They operate as links in the chain that binds Rose's desires and fears to a presence in the basement and to an irrevocable acknowledgment of the division between herself and Bert. The latter is what is important and perceivable. The other factors are important only in bringing about that acknowledgment for Rose and Bert. The ever-imminent confrontation between the two sides of her personality finally manifests itself in a clash that cannot provide a solution. Both Bert and Riley are essential to Rose, but they also manifest incompatible demands.

The play is built around a series of polarities between light and dark, warmth and cold, cosiness and inhospitability, man and woman, husband and wife, domination and subordination, Rose's fears and Rose's desires, and finally Bert and Riley. This final confrontation synthesizes the others.

What is important about the others indicates what is vital about Bert versus Riley. They signify choices defined by their incompatibility, by the fact that they are opposite. We are given no indication of the possibility of a solution for Rose because her desires are defined in opposition to what she already has; they are not pinned down to concrete issues recognizable in other than these relative terms. Rose longs for alternatives—no more and no less. No possible relationship could enable her to express all the range of her individuality all the time. Every relationship is a compromise, and every compromise potentially unstable. Rose's attempts to stabilize the compromise between herself and Bert involved the contemplation of alternatives. This in turn led to the savoring of alternatives and eventually to the collapse of their previous compromise. The conflict between the social need for compromise and the individual need for something more is at the heart of the play, and it is this which we referred to earlier as the "something about the nature of the individual that is incompatible with the communities of men."

In another age Dr. Johnson wrote: "some desire is necessary to keep life in motion, and he whose real wants are supplied, must admit those of fancy." Rose's "real wants" are never established and are never met because she does not know them and could not achieve them, anyway. "Fancy" is nonetheless rampant and nonetheless destructive. Riley functions primarily as an embodiment of Rose's fantasized alternatives to the dissatisfactions of her life with Bert. But in reaching for the alternative she loses what is indispensable in what she already has. To return once more to Dr. Johnson:

> nature sets her gifts on the right hand and on the left. Those conditions, which flatter hope and attract desire, are so constituted, that, as we approach one, we recede from another. There are goods so opposed that we cannot seize both, but, by too much prudence may pass between them at too great a distance to reach either. . . . Of the blessings set before you make your choice, and be content.

Rose's inability to rest content with her choice of life with Bert brings on the collapse of that way of life. The conclusion recognizes no alternatives. The curtain comes down with Rose, as at the beginning of the play, faced with a helpless awareness of the inescapable and insupportable, of the indispensable and the unavailable. Progression on one level encounters circularity on another, and what looked like a revivifying change results only in a regressive mutation. Rose and Bert cannot go on as before, but in the absence of alternatives, they must nonetheless go on. It is this situation, not Rose's death, that forms the conclusion of the play.

POSTSCRIPT

Many of the critics who have written about this play have questioned the consistency of its conclusion, and their discussion has tended to center on the character of Riley. Their criticism seems largely unjustified in the light of the interpretation suggested above. Nevertheless, there does appear to be one loose thread that Pinter has not adequately tied up. The connecting motifs, the repeated images, which gradually converge upon the basement and find concrete expression in the person of the Negro, are finally brought into question by one of Riley's remarks. As Leech neatly puts it: "we are conscious of being invited to look for allegory and yet not sufficiently impelled to conduct the search." This urge toward allegorical interpretation is one that is dictated by the needs of puzzled critics rather than by the needs of the play, but Pinter allows a moment of uncertainty to give some justification to such an approach. The enigmatic figure of Riley at one point threatens to develop sufficient identity to arouse questions about his motives, and not just Rose's. Riley's appeals to Rose to come home are general enough for them to function simply as contrasts to Rose's concern for the sheltering characteristics of her current abode. But at one point, his repeated appeals set up a contrast in another area: "I want you to come home;" and "Your father wants you to come home." This contrast begins to deflect attention from Rose's need for an alternative "home" to speculations about who is doing the calling and why. Instead of remaining the simple focus of Rose's needs, Riley begins to develop sufficient individuality to justify questions about *his* attitudes and concerns. This tendency, slight though it may be, has given support to considerations of what "home" might be aside from the characteristics that Rose has defined for it in her various projections of an alternative world. And this, in turn, invites attempts to locate symbolic significance in the darkness, dampness, etc., instead of acceptance of their unspecified but potent significance as contrasts to the restricted life Rose leads in her confining room. But, as Leech points out, the rest of the play simply does not provide the kind of evidence that would support such interpretations.

Pinter himself has revealed a degree of discontent with the presentation of Riley: "I don't think there's anything radically wrong with the character in himself, but he behaves too differently from the other characters: if I were writing the play now I'd make him sit down, have a cup of tea." Whether this would have solved the problem remains a moot point. Nevertheless, Pinter's comment gives some indication of why the loose end was left dangling. The character of Riley seems for a moment to balance unsatisfactorily between two alternative kinds of intruder that Pinter used in plays written at about the same time as this one. In *The Birthday Party*, the new arrivals actively outmaneuver and carry off their victim. In *A Slight Ache*, the newcomer is totally silent and passive and functions solely to catalyze by his presence the destructive elements already present in the victim's psyche. In *The Room*, Riley's function is primarily the latter, but one or two unfortunate remarks invoke the former possibility and add a slight element of uncertainty to the play's conclusion.

What is finally central to the play, however, is not a symbol, a message or a label, but a process: the process of characters grappling with the problems of the self in its relation to others. It would be very difficult to derive any summarizing moral, metaphysical, political, or philosophical messages from the play—except in the very basic sense in which all of these terms can be spread to cover all activity. To put it more precisely, no religious, political, or philosophical system is being expounded or tested by the activities onstage. The process upon which the play focuses is much more local in its genesis and much more universal in its application: "Before you manage to adjust yourself to living alone in your room, you're not really terribly fit and equipped to go out to fight battles." For Rose, this adjustment of the self to its environment is a process of eternal compromise and ever-present risk. Her longing for a "home," for a place where she could synthesize and satisfy all her needs and fantasies, is never satisfied. The attempt to convince herself that she had found it with Bert was always a self-deception. The belief that she could find it with Riley proved equally fallacious. Trapped in a world of unsatisfactory choices where compromise and contest are inescapable, Rose battles her way through relationships that she can neither make do with nor do without. This process, the ever-present stress between the individual and his companions, is the process dramatized by a play that discovers and begins to develop the dramatic possibilities of language used primarily for interrelational concerns. "The meaning of a great deal of speech behaviour is just the combined personal and social forces it can mobilize and direct."

BARBARA KREPS

Time and Harold Pinter's Possible Realities:
Art as Life, and Vice Versa

If we compare plays such as *Silence, Landscape, Monologue*, and *Old Times* with plays such as *The Room, The Birthday Party, A Slight Ache*, or *The Dumb Waiter*, one thing that seems immediately clear is that Harold Pinter has undergone considerable evolution in his career as a playwright. And yet, when we look at the few official statements Pinter has released over the years about the vision that lies behind these plays, what seems to be equally clear is that he has, from the beginning, been concerned with elaborating a single idea. On March 8, 1960, the program brochure for *The Room* and *The Dumb Waiter* contained a printed sheet of paper in which, among other things, Pinter said: "The desire for verification is understandable but cannot always be satisfied. There are no hard distinctions between what is real and what is unreal, nor between what is true and what is false. The thing is not necessarily either true or false; it can be both true and false. The assumption that to verify what has happened and what is happening presents few problems I take to be inaccurate." In an address to drama students at Bristol in 1962, Pinter incorporated this statement into his speech and expanded it:

> I'm speaking with some reluctance, knowing that there are at least twenty-four possible aspects of any single statement, depending on where you're standing at the time or on what the weather's like. . . . Apart from any other consideration, we are faced with the immense difficulty, if not the impossibility, of verifying the

From *Modern Drama* 22, no. 1 (March 1979). © 1979 by the University of Toronto, Graduate Centre for the Study of Drama.

past. I don't mean merely years ago, but yesterday, this morning.
What took place, what was the nature of what took place, what
happened? If one can speak of the difficulty of knowing what in
fact took place yesterday, one can I think treat the present in the
same way. What's happening now? We won't know until tomorrow or in six months' time, and we won't know then, we'll
have forgotten, or our imagination will have attributed quite false
characteristics to today. . . . We will all interpret a common experience quite differently, though we prefer to subscribe to the
view that there's a shared common ground, a known ground. I
think there's a shared common ground all right, but that it's more
like a quicksand. Because "reality" is quite a strong firm word
we tend to think, or to hope, that the state to which it refers is
equally firm, settled and unequivocal. It doesn't seem to be, and
in my opinion, it's no worse or better for that.

In December 1971, Pinter granted an interview to Mel Gussow in connection
with the New York opening of *Old Times*. One thing that emerges from that
interview is that Pinter still had not significantly revised his earlier views
about the slipperiness of time and of the facts that are commonly supposed
to have been fixed in time:

> GUSSOW: From your point of view the literal fact of a meeting
>   or of a sexual realtionship doesn't really matter.
> PINTER: No, it doesn't. The fact is it's terribly difficult to
>   define what happened yesterday. So much is imagined and
>   that imagining is as true as real.
> GUSSOW: Does the possibility that the meeting might not have
>   taken place make the relationship less meaningful?
> PINTER: No. The fact that they discuss something that he says
>   took place—even if it did not take place—actually seems
>   to me to recreate the time and the moments vividly in the
>   present, so that it is actually taking place before your very
>   eyes—by the words he is using. By the end of this
>   particular section of the play, they are sharing something
>   in the present.

In his plays, revues, and sketches, from *The Room* to *No Man's Land*, this
difficulty in verifying "what happened" remains one of Pinter's central
themes, and this problem of verifying the past naturally leads to (or grows
from—in Pinter the two are too closely related for us to make such sepa-

rations) the problem of verifying identity. "What happened?" means asking who a person was, what a person did, who was the person who could do this if this is what was done—or conversely, *if* this person is really this way, could he or she really have done that? As Pinter asks these questions, moreover, he exposes the frustrations and the failure of human communication, and reveals to us in play after play the separation and isolation of the individual. For twenty years these have been Pinter's primary themes. But if the issues he deals with have remained so remarkably constant throughout his two decades as a dramatist, there has been a profound alteration in his understanding of and approach to these issues, making the plays he has produced in the last decade very different in kind from the plays of menace and victimization he wrote in the late fifties and early sixties. And what is it that is so different about them? Ironically enough, it is Pinter's approach to time.

In large part this change in his handling of time was a simple matter of discovering a new technique. For until *The Basement* (a television play written around 1964 and performed in 1967), Pinter continued to raise questions about time that were contradicted by his own use of time as experienced at the moment of the play's performance. His plots wove in and out of and around the equivocations of time, but the vagaries of time so heavily emphasized in his plots were in fact dramatized through the traditions of a theatrical time *so* verifiable that on a technical level Pinter was as temporally rigid as any neoclassicist could have wished. One of the major changes in Pinter's work of the last decade seems to lie, therefore, in his development of a dramatic mode in which form finally reenforces content—an evolution that chronology suggests might possibly have come about because of the work he had begun to do in the film media, where, by the sheer juxtaposition of two frames rolling out in the single context of the film strip, an audience can be made to leap across large gaps in the chronological time of the events projected on the screen. Film, too, with its capacity for presenting time as both external and chronological on the one hand, and internal and very personal (e.g., "flashbacks") on the other, certainly provided practical examples congenial to Pinter's theories as to how time-as-perceived can be artistically manipulated. So, in the plays of his later development, Pinter may have been consciously experimenting with translating certain celluloid possibilities of time to "live" theater.

And yet, even if film could have suggested certain technical possibilities to Pinter, the change we notice in his plays is not simply a mere question of technique; for by the mid-sixties, even a play like *The Homecoming*, which has a strictly straightforward neoclassical time structure, reveals developments in the way plot turns which indicate that Pinter had by then revised somewhat his earlier views on the subjects of identity, isolation, and victimization.

The root causes of the individual's ultimate isolation are quite different, for example, in *Silence, Landscape, Night, Old Times, Monologue,*, and *No Man's Land* from what they were in *The Room, The Dumb Waiter*, and *The Birthday Party*. His early plays show human isolation as a condition imposed from outside, which is undoubtedly why it was spatially defined through the contrast of a room and everything outside the room. There is society, or a nexus of social relationships of various sorts, and then there are the individuals who do not quite fit (for reasons which are never clear either to them or to us), and who are therefore gradually excluded. What we watch, then, in Pinter's early plays is the process of eviction and the struggle against that process on the part of the individual being excluded. Different as each of these characters is, they all tend, when they realize what is happening to them, to respond in the same way: even if they have earlier been hostile towards the source of threat, they try now to placate it, to exercise their charms to find some common territory and make an ally. Stanley tries, but fails, to convince McCann of his love and respect for the Irish; Ben and Gus send up everything they have in the dumb waiter and apologize for the fact that, though they are trying as best they can, they cannot meet all of its requests; Davies, for all the bad treatment he has received at Mick's hands, nonetheless chooses to line up with him, rather than with Aston; Edward offers the matchseller sherry and scotch, reveals his romantic memories of his past and, when he perceives that they are being laughed at, says, "you're quite right, it is funny. I'll laugh with you!" But niceness and the exiles' observance of all the social amenities are not enough to save them., Assumption of the winning manner is only testimony that they are losing, proof of their vulnerability. The pattern is finally broken by Ruth in *The Homecoming*. Ruth will not be bullied. She stands up, first to Lenny, and later to the family; and, after her example, giving in in the face of threat is a gesture not repeated in Pinter's plays.

The victim refuses to be victimized. That is one aspect of the change from Pinter's old models of victimization that we find in *The Homecoming*. But there are really two potential victims in the play. Ruth winds up something in the past. Teddy is a preview of things to come. Ruth puts the cap on the notion of niceness; if she is going to be used, she will strike an advantageous bargain. And as it turns out, she is not, as Max would first have had it, evicted; on the contrary, she fits into their home quite well. Teddy does not, but for the first time in Pinter, it really does not matter to the exile. To be sure, Teddy makes his attempt at homecoming, but by now he is too much a creature of the New World to be very ruffled by the failure of his visit to the Old World. If he is incapable of being a part of his family's home, it seems a matter of little importance to him, because he has no emotional investment in it in the first place:

> There's no point in my sending you my works. You'd be lost. It's nothing to do with the question of intelligence. It's a way of being able to look at the world. It's a question of how far you can operate on things and not in things. I mean it's a question of your capacity to ally the two, to relate the two, to balance the two. To see, to be able to see! I'm the one who can see. That's why I can write my critical works. Might do you good . . . have a look at them . . . see how certain people can maintain . . . intellectual equilibrium. Intellectual equilibrium. You're just objects. You just move about. I can observe it. I can see what you do. It's the same as I do. But you're lost in it. You won't get me being . . . I won't be lost in it.

Teddy is isolated not so much because he is excluded, but because he excludes. He has, after all, been trying to leave since early in act 2. Teddy's aversion to his family is, of course, understandable: they are an unlikeable crew. Only Teddy, intellectually fatuous and emotionally blank, is neither more whole nor more likeable than they are. The secret of Teddy's success— the secret he tells his family they cannot understand—is "how far you can operate on things and not in things." Emotional detachment is his key. His family, unappealing as they are, cannot bring themselves to break away from living under the same roof, awful as living under the same roof can be. Incapable of indifference to one another, they are caught in a complex family web that spins out hostility in place of love. But, as the last scene makes clear, there is also something in it that they need. Teddy, whose self-contained, unemotional way of speaking is a barometer of his personality, is not like them. He is separate. He refuses to be "lost" in "being." What we see in Teddy is hardly a specimen of great-souled humanity, but there is no doubt that his detachment from others at least makes him very safe.

In some respects, Teddy's way had been paved by Aston in *The Caretaker* and by Stella in *The Collection*. But Aston, if he cannot now be hurt, has been hurt; he refuses now to be evicted from his own space and is finally the evictor. Yet he has known what it is like to be an exile, and it is only because of this that he has learned how it is that one protects oneself: "I feel much better now. But I don't talk to people now. I steer clear of places like

that café. I never go into them now. I don't talk to anyone . . . like that."
Stella's is a quite different case, and she is a more complete enigma. We
have no idea why she tells James that she has slept with Bill. As usual in
Pinter, we are free to deduce all sorts of reasons. But in this *ménage à quatre*,
it is not clear whether Stella is the victim or the victimizer or an amalgam
of both. (Pinter himself finally decided that his sympathies lay with Stella,
but only after he had seen the play performed a number of times.) Like
Teddy, Stella finally refuses to be involved, and so she sits stroking her cat
and smiling sympathetically but silently at James, even as he demands her
involvement in his questions. But unlike Teddy, who is incapable of involvement, Stella finally adopts this position because, as we see in the play,
nothing else has worked for her. Lying (if she is lying) did not work; crying
did not work; pleading did not work; marriage has not worked. It seems
now that silence is her best defense. The stage arrangement, with its split
between the house and the flat, makes Stella's isolation clear in the last third
of the play. Harry, Bill, and James are all on one side; Stella is alone on the
other. It is unclear whether this arrangement is cause or effect, or simply a
visual demonstration of a congenital condition between the sexes.

Despite our inability to resolve exactly what did happen between Stella
and Bill two weeks ago at Leeds, *The Collection*, like the plays that preceded
it, remains a very simple exploration of the relationship between time and
identity. The "story" may open up numerous possibilities, but Pinter's handling of time, which he insists on the plot level is so complex, is dramatically
quite conventional. While the four characters are on stage we know who is
where, why they are there, and at what time they are there. But in Pinter's
recent plays, all of this audience security has disappeared.

As I indicated earlier, Pinter first broke away from conventional dramatic time, not in the theater, but on television. As I see it, *The Basement*
achieves in terms of drama what *Finnegans Wake* achieves in terms of the
novel. And yet most critics seem to have missed the radical nature of the
play, because of their misconceptions about what Pinter is doing in it with
time.

Until *The Basement*, Pinter's plays were firmly planted in the objective
world of space and time. But with *The Basement*, the audience are not aware
until well into the drama—if, indeed, they are ever aware—that none of this
is "really" happening, that the whole thing, or most of it, is a fantasy, or a
dream, or a memory that is being acted out in Law's head. Of course, there
are some strange things which go on almost from the beginning, but Pinter's
ability to present the extremely unusual as nonetheless perfectly possible
initially takes us in. It is strange, of course, that Stott should leave Jane

standing out in the rain when he enters Law's flat, though it is just as strange that the two men who seem to have been best friends should have had absolutely no contact in over ten years. Yet neither situation is impossible or even improbable. Much stranger is Jane's undressing in front of Law only minutes after they have been introduced:

> JANE *begins to take her clothes off.*
> *In the background* STOTT *moves about the room, turning off the lamps.*
> LAW *stands still.*
> STOTT *turns off all the lamps but one, by the fireside.*
> JANE *naked, gets into the bed.*
> LAW: Can I get you some cocoa? Some hot chocolate?
> STOTT *takes his clothes off and, naked, gets into the bed.*
> LAW: I was feeling quite lonely, actually. It is lonely sitting here, night after night. Mind you, I'm very happy here. Remember that place we shared? That awful place in Chatsworth Road? I've come a long way since then. I bought this flat cash down. It's mine. I don't suppose you've noticed the hi-fi stereo? There's all sorts of things I can show you.

This is pretty bizarre behavior even in the most bohemian of circles, and, together with Jane and Stott's obstinate silence at this point, ought to be a give-away clue to what Pinter is doing in this play. But the fact is that it has not been so regarded. Audiences, after all, depend on the characters to give them some indication of what is "normal" in their world, and as Law in no way reacts as if there were anything unusual about his guests' lack of inhibitions, we tacitly conclude that these are three uninhibited but still essentially normal people. And though the situation is certainly a bit strange, it *is* entirely possible. Indeed, we cannot be sure whether this much "really" happened and whether it is this public display of private erotic possession which (together with suggestions from *The Persian Manual of Love*, which Law resumes reading) gives rise to Law's subsequent fantasies, or whether it is in fact *The Persian Manual of Love* itself which, from the beginning, causes Law to imagine all of the events which follow.

Thus, what happens in *The Basement* is entirely, or mostly (depending on where we locate the start of the fantasizing), Law's own construction. The same, therefore, is necessarily true of time. Most of Pinter's critics talk about *The Basement* as a continuation of the old theme of the room, of Law's displacement from it, and of his struggle to regain it. That is, of course, what happens in Law's head. But the standard interpretation makes *The Basement* old stuff for Pinter, whereas it is really a new development. For the crucial thing about this play is not Law's definition in space, but his definition in time. And an important corollary of Law's personal time structure is that, as it is he who peoples his loneliness, he—like the artist—creates, defines, and destroys relationships as a private act of imagination. As they come into his mind, Jane and Stott really exist for Law, just as they really exist on the stage, and really exist for those critics who have not seen them as creatures of Law's fantasies. And because this is so, the truth or falseness of their objective existence in material reality is consequently—as far as Law's perceptions are concerned—quite beside the point; for as Pinter explained to Gussow, "So much is imagined and that imagining is as true as real."

Television provided Pinter with a medium capable of freeing him from the conventional notions of time that he had long been trying to refute. Until *The Basement*, his plays had been saying one thing about time and the verification of fact, while dramatically he had continued to give his plays quite traditional time structures. Television and film, however, seem to have suggested a technique which he has subsequently brought to the theater. In *Silence* and in *Old Times*, we move with no dramatic preparation between past and present; we are left to our own devices to resolve, as best we can, whether the particular phenomenon we are witnessing is memory, instant re-creation of the past, or madness.

In act 1 of *Old Times*, Anna says to Deeley: "There are some things one remembers even though they may never have happened. There are things I remember which may never have happened but as I recall them so they take place." Anna sees herself here as the creator of time, and therefore of the identities which are created in the process of creating time. All through the play, she and Deeley engage in a memory contest in which each one of the two hopes to emerge victorious as the creator of Kate. They have, however, distinctly different approaches to that creation. Deeley is an egocentric fool who, throughout the play, sees all existence only as it filters baldly and unimaginatively through his own ego, and he has for that reason the crudest of approaches to Kate's identity, making "categorical pronouncements" which are, of course, "*my* categorical pronouncement" (emphasis added):

> Myself I was a student then, juggling with my future, wondering should I bejasus saddle myself with a slip of a girl not long out of her swaddling clothes whose only claim to virtue was silence but who lacked any sense of fixedness, any sense of decisiveness,

but was compliant only to the shifting winds, with which she went, but not *the* winds, and certainly not *my* winds, such as they are, but I suppose winds that only she understood, and that of course with no understanding whatsoever, at least as I understand the word, at least that's the way I figured it. A classic female figure, I said to myself, or is it a classic female posture, one way or the other long outworn.
Pause.
That's the position as I saw it then. I mean, that is my categorical pronouncement on the positon as I saw it then.

Anna makes it quite clear that she sees herself—and wants to be seen—as a more altruistic creator than Deeley, and is therefore a finer being:

I found her. She grew to know wonderful people, through my introduction. I took her to cafes, almost private ones, where artists and writers and sometimes actors collected, and others with dancers, and we sat hardly breathing with our coffee, listening to the life around us. All I wanted for her was her happiness. That is all I want for her still.

But in the process of this contest between Anna and Deeley about who was what to whom, both have made Kate indispensable to their notions about their own pasts, and therefore to their notions about themselves and their importance. The final victor in that contest, for which Deeley and Anna have set up the terms, is prefigured long before the final scene. Anna and Deeley discuss at length who will be better able to dry Kate off when she finally emerges from her bath, as the question of who ought really to possess Kate's body (the husband or the lesbian) hovers just at the surface of their conversation. But when Kate reappears, she has already dried herself off. It turns out here, as it is to turn out at the end of the play, that neither husband nor friend is necessary. And so it is that in the last minutes of the play, Anna's cryptic words about memory and creation in act 2 are unexpectedly illuminated as they fly back in her face in an ironic and unforeseen demonstration of just how right she was. For Kate, whom Anna and Deeley have both been pushing as the central figure in the definitions of their own pasts, remembers that one was dead and that she buried or married the other. She waits—significantly—before adding with eloquent ambiguity, "Neither mattered." Without realizing it, therefore, Deeley and Anna have been, literally and metaphorically, bedfellows. In the room with two beds, Kate always slept alone in one. At different times, Anna and Deeley have occupied the other. But when, after Deeley has slept in Anna's bed, he asks who has slept there before him, Kate responds with as much significance for Deeley as for Anna: "No one at all." What is clear by the end of the play is that no one of the three characters is capable of disinterested involvement with any of the others. But Deeley and Anna are more vulnerable than Kate, because they insist on seeing her as an extension of themselves, and thus depend on her to validate their own self-conceptions. Hence, Kate the silent is the strongest of the three, for she lives alone and self-sufficient in a private world to which neither husband nor friend is admitted any farther than the periphery. And because they had seen themselves as central to her life, she—not they—finally has the power both to create and to destroy. She can bury or marry, but whichever it is, she herself remains untouched. For whether it was burial or marriage, husband or friend, it does not matter: her own existence is separate from theirs. And from her separateness, Deeley and Anna—who have deceived themselves about their own natures—are forced to learn about their own isolation.

Involvement is shunned in Pinter's early dramas, not because it is impossible, but because it is potentially threatening. "We're very quiet," Rose says. "We keep ourselves to ourselves. I never interfere. I mean, why should I? We've got our room. We don't bother anyone else. That's the way it should be." Pinter's early victims all subscribe to Rose's philosophy. In a hostile world, safety seems to lie in retreat. But as it turns out, retreat never works. The closed doors are always opened sooner or later, and the past always catches up. Since he has come to insist on the personalization of time, what Pinter now shows us instead is how closed off personality really is.

Before Pinter began to integrate the questions of time into the structures of his drama, his characters continually asked, with portentous voices, "What time is it?" The question, usually a *non sequitur*, called attention to itself for that very reason, and almost always sounded far more like a threat than an idle inquiry after the position of two hands on a watch. The mysterious "menace" that was once Pinter's hallmark is never very clearly motivated, but as the central victims of these early plays are gradually pushed towards isolation and defeat, this menace is often linked with the unresolvable secrets of personal history buried in time past. As Pinter's depiction of time has moved from external to internal, his perceptions about the nature of violence and of isolation have undergone modification. But violence has not therefore disappeared from Pinter's work. It has only lowered its voice.

In some respects, Pinter's earlier vision was more comforting. We could go away from his plays and pin the rap on "the hostile forces latent in society," "the fragmentation of modern man," "society's antagonism to the individual," and so forth. At this stage of the twentieth century, such sentiments have become pretty threadbare with repetition, but behind the dismal vision there was at least a small crumb of consolation: if failure is a given, there is some comfort in thinking it is not our fault. Pinter stopped letting us think that rather early. Edward is, after all, a most unengaging character, and few of us would like to identify with him. Davies is mean of spirit and deserves eviction long before the papers are served on him. And yet, because these two are so vulnerable, we still feel some measure of pity for them at the end.

Nothing like that pity is provoked by Pinter's most recent plays, a lack which is itself a testimony to the kind of isolation Pinter has begun to depict. His vision of a world that contains inexplicable forces of aggression that could destroy us at any minute has been replaced by the view that the individual is ultimately incapable of being touched by any world that is not self-defined. Shared time is a myth. And because of that fact, everything that is shared in it is also a myth. Pinter's world is bounded no longer by doors, but by ego. Doors can be shut, but they can also open—and in Pinter they usually do. Ego is a much safer closure: we open in always on the "I" referent. The terror of Pinter's vision is much subtler now than it was, for it lies not in the fear that comes from his characters making startling and unwanted contact, but in the growing conviction that the human impulse for contact cannot be satisfactorily met. Indeed, his "safest" characters are never touched by that impulse.

Partial connections to something other than "me" are still sometimes made in Pinter, but as when "Ellen moves to Rumsey" (*Silence*) or "Bates moves to Ellen," the connection is never complete, nor is it final. The impulse and the need may both be there, but the characters remain nonetheless confined to their separate areas of the stage, moving back and forth only within private times of their own creation. Love fails, for reasons that are never explained. But in Pinter's recent world, we suspect that Beth's case is typical; when she talks of love, the dominant pronouns are "I," "me" and "my":

> He lay above me and looked down at me. He supported my
>   shoulder.
> *Pause.*
> So tender his touch on my neck. So softly his kiss on my
>   cheek.
> *Pause.*
> My hand on his rib.

Pause.
So sweetly the sand over me. Tiny the sand on my skin.
Pause.
So silent the sky in my eyes. Gently the sound of the tide.
Pause.
Oh my true love I said.

If, as Pinter seems to suggest here at the end of *Landscape*, our truest love is ourself, the logical extension of this view is *Monologue*, where a single character talks to an empty chair, evoking identities that alternately cross back and forth between private hatred and competition, and public sharing and brotherhood.

We laugh as we are supposed to when the Man announces to the chair, "The thing I like, I mean quite immeasurably, is the kind of conversation, this kind of exchange, this class of mutual reminiscence." But the image also capsulizes the point which has underlain all of Pinter's drama since *The Basement*. It is an image highly conscious of itself as image; it invites perception of itself as sheer artifact. As Pinter's plays have moved farther and farther away from anything like stage naturalism, there has been a corresponding increase in the plays' overt self-consciousness, through structures and images which call attention to the fact that they *are* structures and images. And Pinter knows that his breaches of traditional dramatic structures work. "I'm a front-runner," the Man says in *Monologue*:

> My watchword is vigilance. I'm way past mythologies, left
>   them all behind, cocoa, sleep, Beethoven, cats, rain, black
>   girls, bosom pals, literature, custard. You'll say I've been
>   talking about nothing else all night, but can't you see, you
>   bloody fool, that I can *afford* to do it, can't you appreciate
>   the irony? Even if you're too dim to catch the irony in the
>   words themselves, the words I have chosen myself, quite
>   scrupulously and with intent, you can't miss the irony in
>   the tone of *voice*!
> *Pause.*
> What you are in fact witnessing is freedom. I no longer
>   participate in holy ceremony.
> The crap is cut.

In many respects, *No Man's Land*, Pinter's most recent play, breaks with the trends that can be identified in the plays that followed *The Basement*. *No Man's Land* seems rather to be a throwback to his earlier work. We recognize as familiar, for example, the violent threats, the name game, the attempt (on Spooner's part) to enter into a defined territory, and the defensive moves by which Foster and Briggs seek to exclude Spooner; on a technical level, the play returns to neoclassical dramatic time structures (the play takes place in less than twelve hours) and to a more naturalistic type of plotting (which had been left behind in *Silence*, *Landscape*, and *Monologue*). But though *No Man's Land* may recall the techniques and devices of *The Birthday Party* and *The Room*, the play is still significantly closer to *Monologue* than it is to the earlier dramas. Beyond the contempt which is so obvious, the passage quoted above also illustrates something else, for the lone character of *Monologue* is aware—and insists that we be aware—of art's intervention in his existence. Words and tone of voice have been chosen: the Man knows that and tells us that he knows that. It is this consciousness of art at work that *No Man's Land* shares with *Monologue*. At different times in both plays, the characters tell us that they must be perceived in different ways that are, however, not separate but simultaneous. On the one hand, they insist on the real dimensions of their lives, telling us about the past that has preceded them before they have arrived on the stage for their hour in the theater (so that they are entitled, through the "willing suspension of disbelief" that is part of the tradition of stage naturalism, to be seen as "real" characters—entitled, that is, to the same kind of credibility about their existences that we extend to Oedipus, to Hamlet, to Saint Joan); but at the same time that they tell us about the incidents of their past (which confer on them a "real" existence beyond their stage existence as the imaginary beings that they "really" are), they also call attention to the artificer who makes the choices about what and who they are while they are on stage. In other words, they make us straddle a blurry line in our perceptions of them, between acceptance of them as real characters into whose private lives we have been admitted through the stage convention of the missing fourth wall, and awareness of them as artifacts indebted for whatever life they have to an artistic consciousness (in the manner of Pirandello) beyond their own. Foster knows that he has been called for the occasion, and he appreciates the chance to serve:

> A famous writer wanted me. He wanted me to be his secretary, his chauffeur, his housekeeper, his amanuensis. How did he know of me? Who told him? . . .

> I find the work fruitful. I'm in touch with a very special intelligence. This intelligence I find nourishing. I have been nourished

by it. It's enlarged me. Therefore it's an intelligence worth serv-
ing. I find its demands natural. Not only that. They're legal. I'm
not doing anything crooked. It's a relief. I could so easily have
been bent. I have a sense of honour. It never leaves me. Of service
to a cause.

But he also realizes, as artifact, that he serves the needs of the artist and
gives him back the life that has been given: "Listen, my friend. This man
in this chair, he's a creative man. He's an artist. We make life possible for
him. We're in a position of trust."

References to art and the figure of the artist, as well as self-conscious
artifice, have become increasingly evident in Pinter's plays ever since *The
Basement*; but though these signals that call attention to art are new, they are
also logical outgrowths of the beliefs about the relationship between reality
and perception that Pinter has held since the beginning of his career. Art
and reality have never been entirely separate phenomena for him. For if
perception and point of view can change reality, perception creates reality;
reality is thus an artifact, subject—like all works of art—to different interpretations by different perceivers (or to different interpretations at different
times by the same perceiver). The solitary nature of the mind leaves perception, imagination, and memory free to function on the "facts" of every
life in the same way that they function on both the creation and apprehension
of art. In other words, the uncertain boundaries between where reality ends
and art takes over in the creation of life, either in the public theater or in
the privacy of one's own rooms, are determined by the existential fact of
isolation. We are alone with what we perceive. And, like Spooner's unpainted
picture of "The Whistler," what we perceive depends on where we are sitting
and on what the weather is like—and remains unverifiable through the
endeavors of either art or memory.

GUIDO ALMANSI

Harold Pinter's Idiom of Lies

Were I to trace with the firm hand of a surveyor or an accountant the graph of Harold Pinter's progress, or regress, or dramatic itinerary, from the early works to his latest plays, a few trends would emerge: a progressive baring of the symbolic superstructure; new disguises of a violence which becomes purely verbal or goes underground; monologues spreading, following some Beckettian suggestions, while stichomythia, which reached its apex with the interrogation of Stanley in *The Birthday Party*, recedes; intensification of pauses and silences, becoming the natural repositories of meaning (for instance in *The Basement*, *Landscape* and *Silence*, respectively of 1967, 1968 and 1969). But the fundamental element, language, has hardly changed. From *The Room* (written in 1957) to *Betrayal* (performed in 1978), Pinter has systematically forced his characters to use a perverse, deviant language to conceal or ignore the truth. In twenty years of playwriting he has never stooped to use the degraded language of honesty, sincerity, or innocence which has contaminated the theatre for so long. Nor did Pinter have to wait for his own maturity as a dramatist before he acquired the language of deceit and meretriciousness (as often happens with writers who only reach a strategic idiom after a first juvenile production of free-wheeling expressionism). His language was never chaste, but corrupt from birth. In his plays, even the virginal page protected by its candour is polluted, for the blank space conveys evil intentions and vile meanings. Pinter's idiom is essentially human because it is an idiom of lies.

From *Contemporary English Drama* (Stratford-upon-Avon Series 19). © 1981 by Edward Arnold (Publishers) Ltd., 1981.

Irving Wardle in a celebrated article suggested that Pinter's characters ought to be analysed from an ethological perspective, as humanized animals fighting for territory (the room in *The Room*, *The Caretaker*, *The Basement*; the boarding house in *The Birthday Party*; the old house of *The Homecoming*; the flat of *No Man's Land*) rather than for sex, or power, or pleasure, or glory, or immortality. But although the Pinterian hero is often as inarticulate as a pig, stumbling pathetically on every word, covering a pitifully narrow area of meaning with his utterances, blathering through his life, he does not, like any honest animal, seem to whine or grunt or giggle or grumble to give an outlet to his instincts, desires, passions or fears. He grunts in order to hide something else. Even when he grunts—"Oh, I see. Well, that's handy. Well, that's . . . I tell you what, I might do that . . . just till I get myself sorted out."—This grunt is a lie. Pinter's characters are often abject, stupid, vile, aggressive: but they are always intelligent enough in their capacity as conscientious and persistent liars, whether lying to others or to themselves, to hide the truth if they know truth's truthful abode. They are too cunning in their cowardice to be compared to noble animals. They are perverted in their actions and speech: hence human.

On the traditional stage, characters use dialogue for their underhand strategy, but reveal their true selves in monologues. This is not true of Pinter's plays, where both dialogue and monologue follow a fool-proof technique of deviance. You can trust his characters neither when they are talking to others nor when they are talking to themselves: this is what makes *Landscape*, *Old Times*, *No Man's Land* such difficult plays. Characters shift position crab-like, move forward like knights on a chessboard, an oblique tentative step rather than a bold progress. In Pinter's games players do not advance towards their goal (except for the kill, as in Spooner's final speech in *No Man's Land*): they dribble. This requires a picklock-language, used askew, whose crooked insinuation—penetrating between the reality of the *thing* and the reality of the *word*—mocks the straight approach of the honest key.

With Pinter, expression is no longer the specular reflection of an emotion nor the *word* of a *thing*: the mirror is slanted, and the expression therefore does not reflect the opposite and apposite emotion but the adjacent one, so that each sound and image is systematically distorted (Robert to Emma: "I've always liked Jerry. To be honest, I've always liked him rather more than I've liked you. Maybe I should have had an affair with him myself. (*Silence*) Tell me, are you looking forward to our trip to Torcello?") The stage—and the post-Shavian English stage in particular—was used to a perpendicular language, reflecting the inner world of mind and heart with geometric inevitability. Pinter replaced the right angle by an obtuse angle, so that repartees do not rebound directly; this is his special effect which gives the odd ring to his conversations. Not the language of thinking robots, like Shaw's; not the language of men aping apes, like Artaud's; not the language of hysterical clowns, like Ionesco's; not the language of existential preoccupations, like Beckett's: his is a language of hide-and-seek, human/inhuman ("*Inhuman*: the characteristic quality of the human race," Ambrose Bierce). Pinter's world is plausible and understandable in so far as everyone attempts not to be understood.

Yet, in a sense, Pinter's characters do behave like beasts. Their language articulates the three basic survival techniques of animals; fight, flight and mimetism. Stanley, Davies, Teddy, Spooner, Jerry use language either to attack, or to retreat, or to disguise what they are (and what they are is neither here nor there, to crack the wind of a poor pun). In some often quoted statements from early speeches and interviews, Pinter attempted to distinguish himself from the Absurdist tradition by shifting the issue from the difficulty of communication to the danger of communication:

> I think we communciate only too well, in our silence, in what is unsaid, and that what takes place is continual evasion, desperate rearguard attempts to keep ourselves to ourselves. Communication is too alarming. To enter into someone else's life is too frightening, to disclose to others the poverty within us is too fearsome a possibility.

Sincerity, honesty, linguistic generosity, openness, are diabolical inventions that must be shunned because they create chaos. Survival is based on a policy of reciprocal misunderstanding and misinformation. If we were to choose a straightforward approach, we would be at the mercy of others, or of language itself; or even worse: of ourselves, that part of ourselves we do everything to ignore—and this drive towards self-ignorance is the one intellectual enterprise in which we excel. Nothing is more frightening than making Yakov Petrovitch Golyadkin's ordeal of meeting his doppelgänger on the Fontanka Quay close to the Ismailovsky Bridge into a daily routine. Mirrors are "deceptive" says Bill in *The Collection*, and this is our salvation.

In *Uno, Nessuno e Centomila* (*One, No One and One Hundred Thousand*) by Luigi Pirandello, Vitangelo Moscarda, shaving in the morning, realizes for the first time in his life that his nose is crooked. This means that mirrors are "deceptive": they have either deceived him in the past, when he was thinking of himself as a straight-nosed individual, or they are deceiving him now, as he discovers the crooked nature of his trump. Vitangelo creates a breathing space for himself in the antagonism between his two alter-egos (the straight-nosed Cleopatra of history facing the crooked-nosed Cleopatra of hypothesis), and eventually finds solace and comfort in the serene harbour of madness where all opposites are reconciled. Rimbaud's frightening "Je est un autre" ("I *is* another one"), or Lacan's ironical "L'inconscient, c'est le discours de l'autre" ("The unconscious is the discourse of the Other") require intellectual heroes. Like us, Pinter's characters lack this boldness and continue to pretend to be themselves with thorough and impudent bad faith (think of the supreme bad faith of Deeley in *Old Times*) because they are aware that their secrets are so well hidden that they themselves have forgotten where they are. No one is likely to dig them out: not Goldberg or McCann, who must resort to real violence to *get* at Stanley; not Mick with Davies, or Lenny with Ruth, or Anna with Deeley; not Foster and Biggs either, who are defeated by Spooner's proteanism. "Now-a-days to be intelligible is to be found out," says Lord Darlington in *Lady Windermere's Fan*. But, as usual, Wilde is at his best when he does not really know what he is saying. Pinter, whose style abhors the paradoxical truisms *à la Wilde* (the reference to mirrors in *the Collection* is almost a slip), seems to know what he is doing; he wants characters who are *born* liars, and an audience who mistrust them.

In spite of this, critics seem to refuse their new roles as unbelievers. No matter how improbable the statement, implausible the situation, extravagant the motivation, tall the story, honourable critics ponderously assess and discuss the declarations of the Pinterian character as if they were reliable. Spooner "is acquainted with the impeccably aristocratic Lord Lancer. He is able to organize a poetry reading for Hirst that will include . . . a dinner party at a fine Indian restaurant." Mick dreams "of seeing the derelict house as a luxurious penthouse." "It is made quite clear by Ruth that when Teddy met and married her she was a nude photographic model—and this is widely known as a euphemism for a prostitute." When Davies is invited by Aston to stay, "Mick's jealousy is instantly aroused." "In his anger Mick picks up and smashes the figure of the Buddha which is one of Aston's favourite pieces in the room." "Now there is a serious question as to whether Lenny really did this (belting the old lady in the nose, and kicking her to finish the job) . . . at all, much less with such terrifying indifference." "Mick had believed Davies to be an interior decorator."(!?!) In all these instances, critics give the Pinterian hero a credit that he does not deserve and does not require. I don't think we are supposed to believe that Spooner is acquainted with Lord Lancer; that Mick is jealous and angry; that Ruth was a prostitute; that Lenny met a woman who made him "a certain proposal" and beat her, or that he had kicked the old lady who wanted the mangle removed. Least of all are we expected to believe that Mick believed that Davies was an interior decorator. All we know is that there are characters who are making these statements; not that these statements are valid. The Pinterian hero lies as he breathes: consistently and uncompromisingly. Not to lie is as inconceivable to him as to "eat a crocodile" or make love to a spider. Golderg, Mick, Edward, Ben, Lenny, Spooner, are not just occasionally unreliable: they are untrustworthy by definition, since their words only bear witness to their capacity for speech, not to their past or present experience. Pinter's opus, like Pirandello's, is a long disquisition on the masks of the liar: the liar as the man who panics (Davies, Edward, Lenny, Spooner, Robert); the liar as the man who chats ("I talked too much. That was my mistake," says Aston in *The Caretaker*, act 2; but these words would fit Gus, Duff, Foster). In Pinter mendacity is avoidance of identity; the existential equivalent of our daily avoidance of responsibility.

In a sense this is something new in the western theatre. Traditionally the liar is an identifiable character who can be recognized by his mendacious habits. Maskwell, in Congreve's *The Double Dealer*, Don Garcia, in Alarcon's *La Verdad Sospechosa*, Dorante, in Corneille's *Le Menteur*, Lelio, in Goldoni's *Il Bugiardo*, are typological liars, as distinct in their psychological habit as the Spanish braggart, the old dotard, the sententious scholar (or the vamp with a two-foot long cigarette holder). They come on stage and introduce themselves as liars, in the same way as other characters are presented as merchants, seamen or carpenters. Some are good, experienced, well-trained, professional liars; and among them the best and most heroic is Dorante, a giant among his fellow word-forgers, who is even willing to switch his sentimental allegiance in the last scene of the play in order to be able to tell a further lie. Dorante lies to himself, about his own feelings towards two possible beloved women, Clarice and Lucrèce, so as to lie to others, since his commitment to his art as a liar is greater than his commitment to his heart as a lover.

Pinter's liars are not of the same ilk: since everyone lies, the genuine liar no longer exists. Yet the social and emotional survival of characters still depends on speed: how fast they succeed in running away from themselves (once again we come across Golyadkin who "looked as though he wanted to hide from himself, as though he were trying to run away from himself"). I remember an old 1920s comic film in which an actor, frightened by his own shadow, was running—literally like a horse—in order to escape from the incumbent menace. In Pinter's plays people do not sell their shadow like Peter Schlemihl: they give it away because they are frightened by it, and there is no real desire to get it back. Papers are left in distant Sidcup—surely as memorable a literary location by now as Bartleby's Dead Letter Office at

Washington—and Davies, unwilling to recover them until the weather breaks, cannot even face the remembrance of his birthplace: "I was . . . uh . . . oh, it's a bit hard, like, to get your mind back . . . so what I mean . . . going back . . . a good way . . . lose a bit of track, like . . . you know . . ." (act 2).

The past is either unknowable, or modifiable at will. In *No Man's Land* Hirst and Spooner attempt to control each other through a manipulation of the past. The rich and the poor, the successful man of letters (is he?) and the unsuccessful poet, the parched dipsomaniac and the thirsty beggar, fight for two hours, creating and destroying plausible and implausible backgrounds, inventing different versions of the past in which they had met or not met; known or not known each other; seduced or not seduced their respective wives or lady-friends. The factual truth of these fanciful reconstructions is demoted since what matters is the game of pressures and counterpressures. The recollection or the invention of a second wife, or a different mistress, of a new experience, of another life-style, of different war-years (Hirst: "you did say you had a good war, didn't you?" Spooner: "A rather good one, yes.") are gambits in the social game. Autobiography becomes subservient to the necessity of survival, to the requirements of polemics. The character has been married, or fought a war, or belonged to a Club, or turned into a homosexual or a voyeur, if this item of information can be used to humiliate the opponent. This does not exclude the immediate material advantages that are at stake. In *No Man's Land*, Spooner—not unlike Davies in *The Caretaker*—needs settling down, and is available to any moral, social, or sexual prostitution which will solve his problem. But the density and pungency of the dialogue distract us from the drama of the two men (destitution and squalor for Spooner; for Hirst "the last lap of a race . . . [he] . . . had long forgotten to run" and focuses on the brilliance of the verbal duel rather than on the revelations of anguish and despair. The play is a compromise between the linguistic idiosyncrasy of the characters (especially in the case of Spooner, the aged bohemian whose speech is an exquisite florilegium of revolting clichés) and their personal drama built on psychological emptiness. Spooner and Hirst are linguistic shells made of words words words, but there is nothing inside since a man with two lives has no life of his own; a man with several pasts has no past which belongs to him.

It may be interesting to compare the two major productions of *No Man's Land*: Peter Hall's at the *National Theatre* in London, in 1975, and Roger Planchon's at the *Théâtre de l'Athénée* in Paris, in 1979. Hall insisted on the Pinterian theme of the outsider coming in and the insider going out (as in *A Slight Ache* and *The Basement*). On the one hand, Spooner hopes to find a haven of security in the close space of Hirst's residence (hence the emphasis laid on the luxury of the flat); on the other hand, Hirst dreams of escaping into a land of lakes and waterfalls, which turns into "no man's land" when he is awake: a place "which never moves, which never changes, which never grows older, but which remains forever, icy and silent." Hall's quasi-naturalistic approach is somewhat at variance with the last scene of the play, when litanies, incantations, logical and linguistic games prevail. For instance, when Hirst proposes "to change subject . . . for the last time," the three other characters' ritualistic elaboration on the ulterior meaning of this proposal ("But what does . . . [for the last time] . . . mean?") imposes a symbolic pattern upon the play which is alien to Peter Hall's interpretation. Similarly, John Gielgud's impressive crawling across the stage towards a bottle of whisky or a box of cigarettes does not really fit with this final role as a guru, leading Hirst to his glacial abode. Peter Hall, peerless in the tit-for-tat exchanges and in the parodic treatment of the comedy of manners and sexual innuendoes ("Stella?" "You can't have forgotten." "Stella who?" "Stella Winstansley." "Winstansley?" "Bunty Winstansley's sister." "Oh, Bunty. No, I never see her.") is ultimately defeated by his own ability.

Roger Planchon takes almost the opposite approach, stressing the logical/illogical games/galimatias over the flights of fancy and psychological infightings. His whole production concentrates on Spooner, the tempter, the ambiguous manipulator of symbols, who is not quite a drunken Charon but a soused tourist-guide to no man's land. The different ways in which the two main actors in the Paris production drink their liquor is revealing. Hirst downs his drinks with sharp nervous determination, whereas Spooner obscenely lets his whisky linger for a while in his puffed-up cheeks, and seems to find inspiration for the next twist in his yarn from the internal fumes of alcohol, like a drugged oracle. Planchon lays great emphasis on the Bolsover Street passage, which turns into a description of a second-class hell, a dead-end suitable for unimaginative citizens, while the protagonists fight elsewhere on the border of dream, madness and death:

BRIGGS: He . . . Foster . . . asked me the way to Bolsover
    Street. I told him Bolsover Street was in the middle of an
    intricate one-way system. It was a one-way system easy
    enough to get into. The only trouble was that, once in,
    you couldn't get out. I told him his best bet, if he really
    wanted to get to Bolsover Street, was to take the first left,
    first right, second right, third on the left, keep his eye
    open for a hardware shop, go right round the square,

keeping to the inside lane, take the second mews on the
right and then stop. He will find himself facing a very tall
office block, with a crescent courtyard. He can take
advantage of this office block. He can go round the
crescent, come out the other way, follow the arrows, go
past two sets of traffic lights and take the next left
indicated by the first green filter he comes across. He's got
the Post Officer Tower in his vision the whole time. All
he's got to do is to reverse into the underground car park,
change gear, go straight on, and he'll find himself in
Bolsover Street with no trouble at all. I did warn him
though, that he'll still be faced with the problem, having
found Bolsover Street, of losing it. I told him I knew one
or two people who'd been wandering up and down
Bolsover Street for years. They'd wasted their bloody
youth there. The people who live there, their faces are
grey, they're in a state of despair, but nobody pays any
attention, you see. All people are worried about is their
illgotten gains. I wrote to *The Times* about it. Life at A
Dead End, I called it.

Properly done, the speech is hilarious and terrifying, with the sudden irruption of the irrational (of the metaphysical?) into the realm of the most
banal quotidian preoccupation (how to deliver a parcel in Bolsover Street,
London W.1). For Planchon the key moments of the play were these rit-
ualized speeches: the evocation of the scene in Amsterdam, for example,
which Spooner wants to immortalize in a painting (an absurdist "spot of
time"); or the stupendous cricket metaphor, which must sound even better
in Paris in front of an audience unacquainted with the extravagance of the
technical vocabulary of that sport.

SPOONER: Tell me then about your wife?
HIRST: What wife?
SPOONER: How beautiful she was, how tender and how true.
    Tell me with what speed she swung in the air, with what
    velocity she came off the wicket, whether she was
    responsive to finger spin, whether you could bowl a
    shooter with her, or an offbreak with a leg-break action.
    In other words, did she googlie?

The fact that the names of the four characters, Hirst, Spooner, Foster and
Briggs, belong to four well-known cricketers of the turn of the century is

clearly central to the play, but only an English-born critic could venture into this dark domain. Foreigners like Planchon, and myself, have to bow in awe when faced by the mystery of the universe. Planchon's is a darker *No Man's Land*, since the director stressed the areas of obfuscation, whereas Hall preferred the areas of illumination. As a spectator, I preferred the London production; as a reader, I am more tempted by Planchon's interpretation.

II

No matter how determined the playwright is to stamp out the world of intimate thoughts, memories and desires, it always perversely re-emerges. Behind the skin there is the skull, and inside the skull there are ideas, emotions, feelings, amorous longings. In other words, people continue against all evidence and all decency to be "a bit inner." Pinter is the only writer who has transformed psychological depth and inwardness into an insult. Here are Albert's close friends, in *A Night Out*, talking about his "inner life":

> KEDGE: He's a bit deep, really, isn't he?
> SEELEY: Yes, he's a bit deep. *Pause.*
> KEDGE: Secretive.
> SEELEY (*irritably*): What do you mean, secretive? What are you talking about?
> KEDGE: I was just saying he was secretive.
> SEELEY: What are you talking about? What do you mean, he's secretive?
> KEDGE: You said yourself he was deep.
> SEELEY: I said he was deep. I didn't say he was secretive.

But the sworn enemy of any form of *internal* life is Lenny in *The Homecoming*, who wants to know whether Ruth's *proposal* is a *proposal*, leaving no margin for unexpressed desires or intentions. In the tense exchange with Teddy ("taking the piss" out of him, in Peter Hall's apt definition of the mood of the play), Lenny accuses his brother of the ultimate sin: having a life inside. "Mind you, I will say you do seem to have grown a bit sulky during the last six years. A bit sulky. *A bit inner*. A bit less forthcoming" (act 3, my italics). The adjective *inner* becomes truly offensive, since *innerness* is a defiance against the unwritten laws of common decency which requires one should never say or think anything related to the *inner* life. The "hidden

imposthume" is no longer located in a special point of the rotten body of
the individual or of society; it becomes equivalent to the totality of *inner* life.
Characters are superficial and unfathomable in their superficiality. In his
cruel exchange with Max about his own conception, Lenny mocks the fact
that there could be an emotional or sentimental background—an *inner* motion—behind the copulative act which generated him: "That night . . . you
know . . . the night you got me . . . that night with Mum, what was it like?
Eh? When I was just a glint in your eye. What was it like? What was the
background to it? I mean, I want to know the real facts about my background.
I mean, for instance, is it a fact that I was the last thing you had in mind?"
(act 3). Even if Lenny, because of his own bastardy, was just mocking his
presumed father, as some critics have suggested, the main target of his speech
remains the *inner* life. Pinter's characters long for a world without conscience,
not out of fear that it will "make cowards of us all," but out of laziness.
Thought and feeling are tiresome and demanding.

I have emphasized the novelty of Pinter's exploitation of man's supreme
cultural gift: mendacity. Yet the reference to Hamlet reminds us that, in
another sense, Pinter's use of a beguiling language is not new in the western
theatre. On the contrary, the language of lies may be innate with the theatrical
phenomenon. For Martin Esslin, who has been the sensible and reasonable
chronicler of the unreasonable Absurd, there is a main line of development
in European theatre, "from Sophocles to Shakespeare to Rattigan," where
people on the stage have "always spoken more clearly, more directly, more
to the purpose than they would ever have done in real life." Then dramatists
like Strindberg and Wedekind started to introduce "a certain defectiveness
of communication between characters—who talk past each other rather than
to each other." Finally we get to Chekhov, who inaugurates *The Theatre of
Chatting*, in Alberto Moravia's felicitous formulation. Esslin singles out the
mortuary promise of peace and serenity that Sonia makes to her uncle in
the last scene of *Uncle Vanya* as the point of compromise between a rhetorical
tradition, that wants Sonia's speech more eloquent than it would have been
in real life, and the exigency of obliqueness, so that she pretends to believe
what she does not believe, though aware that no one believes that she believes
what she says she believes (a Dantesque conundrum). Esslin's is a brilliant
reinvention of three thousand years of theatre history from discourse to chat,
from an open game to a closed game, from the language of confession (characters in Greek drama are like Quakers foced to confess their sins in public)
to the language of strategy.

Yet this interpretation ignores irony (the author's, the character's, the
spectator's ironies) without which drama is merely a vulgar metaphor. If we

take into consideration the role and function of irony in western theatre, then theatrical language has alway been strategical. Is it necessary to remind ourselves of the "antic disposition," which is a blueprint for deceit and a licence for self-deceit, or of Shakespeare as the supreme ironist in Kierkegaard's paradoxical definition (for Heine the supreme ironist was God; for Kierkegaard Shakespeare)? If we look at the past history of the theatre from another perspective than the one taken by Martin Esslin, the stage becomes a territory dominated by strategic preoccupations, and its language a language of manoeuvres, not of confrontation. Words have been uttered on the stage with a certain purpose in mind, and it would be wrong to believe that the aim has always been clarification and not obfuscation. I am well aware that before Freud and Heidegger people were stupid and ignorant about obfuscations, since they had not read *Traumdeutung* and *Sein und Zeit*, but even our ancestors had their own occult means of distinguishing between clarity and darkness.

III

If a character in a play says "Mother, give me the sun!," this utterance can be frightening because it is indicative of a deranged mind. Pinter has succeeded in transfering the frightening effect from the extravagance of madness to the banality of normality. He knows how to exploit the disgust of worn-out expressions, making us feel that only a deranged mind would dare to use them. The first hero of repulsive clichés is Goldberg in *The Birthday Party*. His complacent self-satisfied articulation of rotting fragments from a language of null feeling and null sensibility succeeds in creating a full-fledged character, obscene because he uses language at its most common denominator. "Culture? Don't talk to me about culture. He was an all-round man, what do you mean? He was a cosmopolitan." "School? Don't talk to me about school. Top in all subjects. And for why? Because I'm telling you, I'm telling you, follow my line? Follow my mental? Learn by heart. Never write down a thing." Only Max, in *The Homecoming*, reminiscing about his family life, can create such a feeling of revulsion for the utter emptiness of his speech. We laugh at chat, small talk, gabble, because their revelations would be too awesome if we took them seriously (Heidegger is the modern thinker who has dared to contemplate the abyss of Gerede, chatting, and Pinter is his representative on the stage). In *A Night Out*, a much underrated play, conversation viscidly crawls from one pool of slime to the next. The exchanges between the old man and Albert's young friends at the coffee-stall, the dialogue between the two office girls at the party, are a magnificent display of linguistic horrors. There are bubbles of empty speech which explode with dismal dampening effect when Kedge and Seeley comment about a football match:

KEDGE: What's the good of him playing his normal game? He's
   a left half, he's not a left back.
SEELEY: Yes, but he's a defensive left half, isn't he? That's why
   I told him to play his normal game. You don't want to
   worry about Connor, I said, he's a good ballplayer but
   he's not all that good.
KEDGE: Oh, he's good, though.
SEELEY: No one's denying he's good. But he's not all that good.
   I mean, he's not tip-top. You know what I mean?
KEDGE: He's fast.
SEELEY: He's fast, but he's not all that fast, is he?
KEDGE (*doubtfully*): Well, not all that fast . . .
SEELEY: What about Levy? Was Levy fast?

Am I the only reader who finds this fragment of conversation hurtful in its vacuity? Empty chatting possesses an existential fullness, when a comment upon the weather, or about the routine of daily life, is the disguise of a fundamental question: "Do you know that I exist?" or "I do exist. What about you?" Kedge and Seeley are beyond that pale. They fulfill the ultimate structuralist dream: a language that speaks us instead of a language that is spoken by us. The *koine* of the tribe ensnares the characters into a deceptive *distinguo*. The difference between "good" and "all that good," "fast" and "all that fast," gives the speakers the illusion of free will and freedom of speech and choice. They believe that they are in control while they are being controlled. They are the puppets of language: their *parole* is utterly subservient to the *langue*, which is perversely vacuous and futile.

   In normal life language ranges from a full sensual enjoyment of the phonetic articulation in our mouth, the voicing process in our throat, the mechanics in our brain and nervous system to a purely repetitious production of alien sounds and alien concept, as if the vocal apparatus were merely the loudspeaker of a cheap Hi Fi system. At the one end we have the language evoked by William Gass: "the use of a language like a lover . . . not the language of love, but the love of language, not matter but meaning, not what the tongue touches, but what it forms, not lips and nipples, but nouns and verbs." Or by Jean Genet: "The word balls has a roundness in my mouth." On the other end we chew over and over the language of dead people. It is like the range of salivas in Salvador Dali's celebrated metaphor: "la bave immonde, antigéométrique du chien" ("the lurid, antigeometrical spittle of the dog") vs. "la bave quintessentielle de l'araignée" ("the quintessential spittle of the spider"). Kedge's and Seeley's phonation resembles a form of articulatory rumination. In their mouth they masticate the dessiccated saliva which was once in the mouth of an idiot who first *coined* these sentences: and the words of the idiot signify nothing. The two boys' destiny is the triumph of fatuousness: hence it is a tragic destiny. They cannot enjoy their football because they have been denied the linguistic capacity to utter their personal appreciation. Pinter refuses—rightly in my view—to give voice to their inarticulate sounds in the old populist manner: but he gives them an audience.

In the early plays Pinter had been the virtuoso of phonomimesis: a "superrealist," in the sense the word has acquired in the modern art scene. He used to exploit the stammerer: either the phonetic stammerer, or the conceptual stammerer, piling up debris of words, stumps of phrases, truncated fragments of meaningful expressions to barricade the entrance to the nearest burrow where, in a cowardly way, they hid themselves. Martin Esslin effectively sums up the novelty of Pinter's elegant and spectacular illiteracy: "inarticulate, incoherent, tautological and nonsensical speech might be as dramatic as verbal brilliance when it could be treated simply as an element of action." Davies, in *The Caretaker*, was the expert in the art of stuttering acrobatics, interspersed with *Pindaric* flights of stupendous *bad grammar*: "What about them shoes I come all the way to get I hear you was giving away?" These are linguistic *tours de force*, as difficult and as artificial as the sketch of the master skater who pretends to be a clown who pretends not to know how to skate. In the latest plays, however, the treatment of inarticulacy tends to disappear, whilst the texts still manipulate the inane components of small talk as the weaponry of pusillanimous characters (Deeley in *Old Times*, Duff in *Landscape*, Jerry in *Betrayal*). Two new mannerisms come to light: the mannerism of the hard-of-hearing, and the mannerism of the hard-of-understanding.

Hard of hearing:

EMMA: It's Torcello tomorrow, isn't it?
ROBERT: What?
EMMA: We're going to Torcello tomorrow, aren't we?

And in *No Man's Land*:

HIRST: What was he drinking?
SPOONER: What?
HIRST: What was he drinking?
SPOONER: Pernod.

Hard of understanding:

ROBERT: I thought you knew.
JERRY: Knew what?
ROBERT: That I knew. That I've known for years. I thought
    you knew.
JERRY: You thought I knew?

And in *Old Times*:

KATE: Yes, I quite like those kind of things, doing it.
ANNA: What kind of things?
DEELEY: Do you mean cooking?
KATE: All that thing.

Pinter is a maestro in orchestrating not small but minute talk: the almost unnoticeable curves in an evasive conversation (well, all conversations are evasive in Pinter). He successfully strives to create meaning in the most unpromising areas of signification: casual remarks, perfunctory exchanges, usage and abusage of worn-out phrases, absurd observations, gossip, the grating sound of blathering and blabbering, the tittle-tattle of quotidian verbiage.

In the area of the absurd nothing can rival the intimate aggression of the opening line of a text which lures the reader into a territory whose conventions, location, rules, time-scale and habits he ignores. By definition the *incipit* must be shocking and alienating, since it forces us to enter into a dark room without knowing what and whom to expect there. "Who's there?" "Nay, answer me; stand and unfold yourself" (Hamlet, 1.1.1) is no mean example of initial shock. The unsurpassed master in opening gambits in the twentieth century was Ernest Hemingway. Take the initial strategy of *The Light of the World*: "When he saw us come in the door the bartender looked up and then reached over and put the glass covers on the two free lunch bowls." This seems to me supreme; a sense of tactical manoeuvering which is unmatched in modern literature. But since Hemingway's death the insignia of the foremost expert in opening theory—where the author tries to defeat the reader on the chessboard of the text—have been passed on to Harold Pinter. His late plays present a stunning range of dramatic entrances:

The Lover	RICHARD (*amiably*): Is your lover coming today?
	SARAH: Mmnn.
	RICHARD: What time?
Old Times	KATE (*reflectively*): Dark.
	DEELEY: Fat or thin?
	KATE: Fuller than me, I think.
No Man's Land	HIRST: As it is?
	SPOONER: As it is, yes please, absolutely as it is.

This last exchange is *absolutely* untranslatable. Hirst pours a glass of whisky in the *Théâtre de L'Athénée* saying "Tel quel?" And Spooner: "Tel quel. Absolument tel quel." That's not it. And "absolument" is miles away from "absolutely." Gone is the ritual, lost is the effect.

The Pinterian speech often opens with a statement which sounds familiar and yet is already lost, irrevocably alien. Like Freud, Pinter makes the insignificant significant; unlike Freud, Pinter refuses to explain and expand on the forces which govern these transformations. Ruth's "Oh, I was thirsty," after draining a glass of water in *The Homecoming*, is pregnant with signification, and yet impregnable in its mystery. It suggests an avenue of meaning, but declines to open or illuminate it. In other words, Pinter is generous with his reader, contrary to current belief. He allows him to think, and puzzle, and struggle with his own emotional and intellectual imcompetence. Beyond that lies another territory which is more frightening, mysterious and unfathomable: where feelings are uttered, ideas debated, emotions expressed. As Karl Kraus put it, "Nothing is more incomprehensible than the discourse of a person for whom language is only used to make himself understood." This is the ultimate horror, which is the reserve of artists of a different ilk. But Pinter is no Lawrence, is no Conrad. He provides us with the oblique tools to come to terms with our own inadequacy, accept our moral and intellectual cowardice, understand our misunderstanding. He is the unreliable guide to a land of unreliance: hence within his terms of reference he is consistent, persuasive and ultimately trustworthy. Elsewhere one finds the *agents provocateurs* who promise feelings, emotions, passions, desires or even ideas.

ENOCH BRATER

Cinematic Fidelity and the Forms
of Pinter's Betrayal

Pinter's characters in *Betrayal* are boring. Preoccupied with children, home, extramarital affairs, tablecloths, and happinesss, they recite the lines that have been assigned to them as educated, pampered, polite, moderately cultivated, upper-middle-class Londoners. Even their taste in modern literature is as unexceptional as it is predictable. Though they may occasionally feel obliged to read Yeats on Torcello or to take their summer holidays in the Lake District, what they really enjoy are the mundane little novels about ordinary people much like themselves in "the new Casey or Spinks." Here everything is ordered, fixed, and, above all, contained. Life does not pass these people by; it merely goes on for them. "Betrayal" is in this context a rather lofty word for such bourgeois and unimaginative infidelities. For Pinter's people in this play only *think* there is depth to their passions: though their lives are not exactly meaningless, the fact is they are not especially interesting. What is there about this trio, then, that compels us to study in detail every move they make as we reconstruct their sad, sometimes comic, and always ironic chronicle of who-did-what-to-whom, when, where, and under-what-circumstances? To answer these questions we must first take a hard look at some of the dramatic forms Pinter employs so skillfully in this work.

Pinter's drama has for a long time been far more compelling for narration rather than plot. How his story develops is more impressive than the story itself. In *Betrayal*, moreover, it is practically impossible to separate the two.

From *Modern Drama* 24, no. 4 (December 1981). © 1981 by the University of Toronto, Graduate Centre for the Study of Drama.

Every critic, of course, will notice that this particular tale is told (almost) backwards. There are three prominent exceptions to this rule, signified in scenes 2, 6, and 7 by the simple intrusion of the unexpected stage direction "Later." Let us review for a moment the sequence of the scenes in the order in which we see them performed. Scene 1 takes place in the spring of 1977 in a London pub. Emma and Jerry are present. Scene 2 takes place *later* that same spring in the study of Jerry's house. Robert and Jerry are present. Scene 3 takes place in the winter of 1975 at the flat Jerry and Emma have let at #31 Wessex Grove, Kilburn; in this scene, of course, only these two characters are present. Scene 4 takes place in the autumn of 1974 at Robert and Emma's house. This is the first time all three players are on stage at the same time. The scene begins with Robert and Jerry alone (the former summons his wife offstage, who replies, "I'll be down"), and will end with the highly charged emotional impact of Emma in her husband's arms after her lover has departed:

> ROBERT *and* JERRY *leave.*
>   *She remains still.*
> ROBERT *returns. He kisses her. She responds. She breaks away, puts*
>   *her head on his shoulder, cries quietly. He holds her.*

This is also the place where Pinter specified an intermission is possible, literally pulling down the curtain on Emma's affair with her husband's "best man." Scene 5 takes place in the summer of 1973 in a hotel room in Venice. Only Robert and Emma are on stage, but Jerry insinuates himself as the crucial offstage presence in the shape of a critical letter which gets into the wrong hands at American Express:

> To be honest, I was amazed that they suggested I take it. It could never happen in England. But these Italians . . . so free and easy. I mean, just because my name is Downs and your name is Downs doesn't mean that we're the Mr and Mrs Downs that they, in their laughing Mediterranean way, assume we are. We could be, and in fact are vastly more likely to be, total strangers. So let's say I, whom they laughingly assume to be your husband, had taken the letter, having declared myself to be your husband but in truth being a total stranger, and opened it, and read it, out of nothing more than idle curiosity, and then thrown it in a canal, you would never have received it and would have been deprived of your legal right to open your own mail, and all this because of Venetian je m'en foutisme. I've a good mind to write the Doge of Venice about it.

Scene 6 takes place *later* the same summer back at the flat in Wessex Grove and features another duet for Emma and Jerry. For a moment we are back in Venice again: Emma has brought to the flat a tablecloth purchased there while on holiday. Scene 7 takes place *later* yet in the summer of 1973 in an Italian restaurant in London where obligatory posters of Venezia make Emma the key offstage character. Robert and Jerry are on stage, along with the extra who takes the part of the waiter or "his son." Paintings are difficult to see in the theater, but Pinter's waiter calls our attention to this one: "Venice, signore? Beautiful. A most beautiful place of Italy. You see that painting on the wall? Is Venice. . . . You know what is none of in Venice? . . . Traffico." In scene 8 we are back for the last time in Emma and Jerry's flat in the summer of 1971 as the lovers meet again on stage. Scene 9 takes place in the winter of 1968 in the bedroom of Robert and Emma's house. All three principals appear for the second time, but only in the following order; first Jerry is discovered alone, sitting in the shadows; Emma then comes in, is later joined by Robert; and the scene and play end after Robert leaves the room as Emma and Jerry "*stand still, looking at each other.*" Shades of T. S. Eliot: in my beginning is my end. In every scene Pinter has made highly efficient use of his offstage character: the "odd man out" is not really out at all. Two-character scenes are really three-character scenes, for the indirect action of each scene concerns the character who is not on stage at all.

The arrangement of scenes in *Betrayal* is, moreover, deceptively simple. And it is far from being a gimmick. For the three forward movements in time, those that take place in scenes 2, 6, and 7, follow two crucial scenes of direct confrontation with "betrayal." In the opening scene of the play Emma betrays Jerry by implying that she has told her husband about their affair only the night before. This provides the dramatic necessity for the first forward movement, Jerry's confrontation with Robert. Jerry's mortification turns to indignation when he realizes that he has been betrayed not only once, but twice. Emma betrays him the night before when she deliberately misleads him, but Robert has betrayed him for four years by never letting on that he knew about their affair since the trip to Venice in 1973:

> JERRY: Why didn't she tell me?
> ROBERT: Well, I'm not her, old boy.
> JERRY: Why didn't you tell me?
>   *Pause.*
> ROBERT: I thought you might know.
> JERRY: But you didn't know for *certain*, did you? You didn't *know!*

ROBERT: No.
JERRY: Then why didn't you tell me?
  Pause.
ROBERT: Tell you what?
JERRY: That you knew. You bastard.
ROBERT: Oh, don't call me a bastard, Jerry.
  Pause.

Scene 5, which stages the next major confrontation with betrayal, precedes the next two forward movements. Pinter uses the old device of a letter to make Robert aware of the fact that he has been betrayed, a fact Emma coldheartedly confirms:

ROBERT: Was there any message for me, in his letter?
  Pause.
  I mean in the line of business, to do with the world of
  publishing. Has he discovered any new and original
  talent? He's quite talented at uncovering talent, old Jerry.
EMMA: No message.
ROBERT: No message. Not even his love?
  Silence.
EMMA: We're lovers.
ROBERT: Ah. Yes. I thought it might be something like that,
  something along those lines.

The next two scenes move forward in time and show first Emma and Jerry in the flat (scene 6), followed by Robert and Jerry in the Italian restaurant (scene 7). In the first of these two scenes we watch Emma avoid telling Jerry that Robert knows what has been going on:

JERRY: I got your letter.
EMMA: Good.
JERRY: Get mine?
EMMA: Of course. Miss me?

The irony cuts deep when we next see Jerry telling Emma of his "terrible panic" when *her* letter from Venice was temporarily lost:

JERRY: I had a terrible panic when you were away. I was
  sorting out a contract, in my office, with some lawyers. I
  suddenly couldn't remember what I'd done with your
  letter. I couldn't remember putting it in the safe. I said I
  had to look for something in the safe. I opened the safe. It

wasn't there. I had to go on with the damn contract . . . I
kept seeing it lying somewhere in the house, being picked
up . . .

EMMA: Did you find it?

JERRY: It was in the pocket of a jacket—in my wardrobe—at
home.

In the next scene Robert similarly avoids telling Jerry what he now knows
for certain is an act of betrayal:

ROBERT: You know what you and Emma have in common? You
love . . . the new novel by the new Casey or Spinks. It
gives you both a thrill.

JERRY: You must be pissed.

ROBERT: Really? You mean you don't think it gives Emma a
thrill?

JERRY: How do I know. She's your wife.

Pause.

ROBERT: Yes. Yes. You're quite right. I shouldn't have to
consult you. I shouldn't have to consult anyone.

In *Betrayal*, therefore, it is the arrangement of the scenes that makes ironies
accumulate and the drama as a whole possible. It is not so much *what we
know* but *when we know it* that is responsible for the real tension that bristles
so ferociously beneath the contained surface of this work. In scene 1 Emma
does not want Jerry to call her "darling" anymore, though as lovers they
had quite naturally greeted each other with this epithet at the opening of
scene 6. In the same scene Emma tells Jerry that she did not go to Torcello
because "The speedboats were on strike, or something," though in the very
next scene Robert tells Jerry that he went "whoomp—across the lagoon in
the dawn" by speedboat—alone. We are meant to read between the lines;
after all, in the theater we have lived through scene 5. A tablecloth we hardly
notice when we see it in the opening scene defines itself as late as scene 6,
when Emma brings it into the flat as a memento from Italy. And an innocent
poster of Venice is not so innocent after all when Robert and Jerry sip Corva
Bianco beneath it in a publisher's haunt like Bianchi's back in London.
Everything happens, nothing is explained. And when things happen in *Betrayal*, they happen visually rather than verbally. Props are made "to talk,"
time is allowed to speak for itself between the scenes and through costumes
(were miniskirts really that short back in 1968?), and actors communicate to
us in gesture, silence, and pause, all those characteristic Pinter "words" they
never get to recite on stage.

With its emphasis on visual statement, and especially in its concise arrangement of nine short scenes which move so uninhibitedly back and forth in time, *Betrayal* shows more clearly than any previous Pinter play the profound effect his work in the movies has had on his dramatic technique. And although *Betrayal* reads at times like a filmscript, its real originality lies in the way it adapts certain cinematic strategies and makes them functional in terms of theater. *Betrayal* makes us concerned with the unities and disunities of time, with deception and self-deception, with the past in the present and the present in the past. In order to make these themes work on stage, the play must abandon realism's literal conformity to chronological time for the more representative patterning of temporality normally associated with cinematography and film-editing. Several Pinter screenplays use time in ways that establish striking structural precedents for the methods of exposition featured in *Betrayal*. Foremost among these is *Accident*, which Pinter adapted in 1967 from the novel by Nicholas Mosley. This screenplay begins with a scene near the end of its "story," then flashes back to a scene furthest in time—from which point the scenes move forward chronologically with several brief flashbacks until a point in time close to where the opening scene began. Then the closing scene picks up the "story" at precisely the point when the flashback (the bulk of the film) began at the conclusion of the opening scene. *Betrayal*, like *Accident*, also begins at the end of a story. But instead of backward movements embedded in a forward movement (which is itself a flashback), the play has three forward movements in an essentially backward movement. In *The Pumpkin Eater*, which Pinter adapted from the novel by Penelope Mortimer in 1964, time is manipulated much as it is in *Accident*. The opening scene is in the present. Then without dramatic preparation the next scene flashes back ten years. The following eight scenes move backward and forward within the ten-year flashback before reestablishing the "story" in the present, as in the opening scene. *The Go-Between*, from the Hartley novel, uses a far simpler time framework. We begin in the present, flash back to the past (where everything takes place chronologically), and then return to the present for the final brief scene of the film.

But in theater everything is more difficult. We must rely on men and women, on actors, not on any machine. "[T]he theatre's much the most difficult writing for me," Pinter admitted, "the most naked kind, you're so entirely restricted."

> Televison and films are simpler than the theatre—if you get tired
> of a scene you just drop it and go on to another one. (I'm exag-

gerating, of course.) What *is* so different about the stage is that you're just *there*, stuck—there are your characters stuck on the stage, you've got to live with them and deal with them.

Juggling time on stage is always an awkward business. Stage sets need to be moved in and out, costumes need to be changed, and actors need to build their characters backward rather than forward. For in the theater the order in which the events are staged is the only order in which the material will enter our consciousness. There is no film editor to "arrange" the incidents differently for us on celluloid clips. In *Betrayal* Pinter has set about to adapt cinematic time and make it work within the limitations imposed by concrete stage space. What results is a new kind of drama for Pinter, one that liberates him from a stuck-in-the-room tableau at the same time that it allows the past to speak for itself without the vagaries—not to mention the pathologies—of any character's memory.

Up to this point we have been talking about the most obvious influence of Pinter's career as screenwriter on the structure of *Betrayal*, the arrangement of its scenes. These, like filmed "shots," are broken into nine discrete units which order time for the exigencies of the drama rather than the beating of a clock. But what is perhaps more important to notice about this play is the way the past has been subjected to an "objective" point of view, a cinematic documentation of the forms of betrayal. In earlier Pinter works for the stage we learn about the past only as the characters tell us about it: their imaginings, always inseparable from reality, are in performance "as true as real." They are also the only testimonies about the past that the earlier drama will enigmatically supply. But in *Betrayal* the past speaks for itself: no character is permitted the luxury of coloring the action that might or might not have taken place before the curtain goes up on these sets. The typology of double-dealing is currently staged for us in a factual presentness that takes place before our very eyes. We are literally looking through the fourth wall, in this case peeking voyeuristically through the proverbial keyhole, so to speak. No longer is the past recaptured, recycled, and reinterpreted through memory. Instead, it is invented for us and staged as documentary evidence which we are then obliged to "judge" for ourselves. The initial image of *Betrayal* was, in the playwright's own words, "Two people at a pub . . . meeting after some time." In an interview Mel Gussow asked Pinter why he decided "*to go backward in time instead of forward as usual.*" Pinter replied: "After I found out what they were talking about. They were talking about the past. So, I thought I'd better go back there."

GUSSOW: In *Old Times*, you stayed right in the present. You
     didn't show us what happened. You talked about what
     might have happened.
PINTER: In this case, when I realized the implications of the
     play, I knew there was only one way to go and that was
     backwards. The actual structure of the play seemed to
     dictate itself. When I realized what was going on, this
     movement in time, I was very excited by it.

In *Betrayal* characters do talk about the past, but only reluctantly. They are
hardly the same loquacious personalities we remember from *Old Times* and
No Man's Land.

EMMA: Well, it's nice, sometimes, to think back. Isn't it?
JERRY: Absolutely.
     Pause.
     How's everything?
EMMA: Oh, not too bad.
     Pause.Do you know how long it is since we met?
JERRY: Well I came to that private view, when was it—?
EMMA: No, I don't mean that.
JERRY: Oh, you mean alone?
EMMA: Yes.
JERRY: Uuh . . .
EMMA: Two years.
JERRY: Yes, I thought it must be. Mmnn.
     Pause.
EMMA: Long time.
JERRY: Yes, it is.
     Pause.
     How's it going? The Gallery?

In this opening scene the effort is to suppress the past, to use words to
conceal rather than reveal what both characters know is too unpleasant to
remember. Jerry and Emma repeatedly assured each other that they are
"fine." Yet we subsequently discover that he has a hangover and that her
marriage collapsed the night before. The implication here seems to be that
in this play the past is going to have to speak for itself. For example, in this
short exchange reference is made to a scene that Jerry would rather not talk
about, though Emma tempts him to "think back." He changes the subject
by asking her about something neutral, something he is not really interested

in, her work in the Gallery. It is not until scene 3, two years before in their flat in Wessex Grove, that we learn why Jerry avoids saying much about their last meeting alone. For the scene that he refuses to uncover presents the bitter end of their affair. It is the scene where keys on symbolic rings are returned; they can be "Green" no longer. And so Emma's inevitable closure: "Thanks. Listen. I think we've made absolutely the right decision." Stage directions: "*She goes. He stands*"—alone. Curtain.

In staging the past as documentary history, *Betrayal* again shows its relationship to a filmscript like *Accident*. For when Pinter adapted Mosley's work for the screen, he changed the entire fictional point of view. In the novel the bulk of the story, the entire flashback, is narrated from the perspective of its main character, Stephan. But Pinter did not present these episodes from an introspective, private, or subjective point of view. He fixed the action, instead, in real, objective time rather than in psychological time. As Pinter explained so well, the attempt to match images to every turn of Stephan's thought would result in an overwrought film, far too literary in the sense that everything would be overexplained. In an interview with John Russell Taylor, Pinter discussed his decision to strip *Accident* of its subjective form:

> At first we thought of perhaps trying to do it the way the book does, to find a direct film equivalent to the free-association, stream-of-consciousness style of the novel. I tried a draft that way, but it just wouldn't work—anyway, I couldn't do it. You see, suppose a character is walking down a lane . . . You could easily note down a stream of thought which might be perfectly accurate and believable, and then translate it into a series of images: road, field, hedge, grass, corn, wheat, ear, her ear on the pillow, tumbled hair, love, love years ago . . . But when one's mind wanders and associates things in this way it's perfectly unselfconscious. Do exactly the same thing on film and the result is precious, self-conscious, over-elaborate—you're using absurdly complex means to convey something very simple. Instead, you should be able to convey the same sort of apprehension not by opening out, proliferating, but by closing in, looking closer and closer, harder and harder at things that are there before you.

In *Betrayal*, as in *Accident*, Pinter goes back to the past for a close look at the incidents which rightly serve as indexes for actual experience. Subjective memory, the way we learn about the past in the earlier stage plays, is always unreliable in this respect. And adapting a cinematic form means that Pinter will not run the risk of repeating what he has done before. For in *Old Times* and *No Man's Land* he had already succeeded in dramatizing the impossibility of verifying the past:

> [We] are faced with the immense difficulty, if not the impossibility, of verifying the past. I don't mean merely years ago, but yesterday, this morning. . . . A moment is sucked away and distorted, often even at the time of its birth. We will all interpret a common experience quite differently, though we prefer to subscribe to the view that there's a shared common ground, a known ground. I think there's a shared common ground all right, but that it's more like a quicksand.

In *Betrayal* the past is finally verified for us because an objective "camera" eye can be brutally, inhumanly honest. Cold rather than calculating, it reveals the virtual past without the intrusion of what a psychologist would call screen memory. In view of the records it offers, the characters in this play are woefully inept at documenting their own history. In scene 1, for example, and repeatedly through the play, Jerry recalls playfully tossing Emma's daughter Charlotte up in the air, but he fails, as Emma points out, to remember that he did it in *his* kitchen, not hers. And in scene 3 Jerry— perhaps even Emma—has difficulty remembering when they were last at their flat:

> EMMA: Can you actualy remember when we were last here?
> JERRY: In the summer, was it?
> EMMA: Well, was it?
> JERRY: I know it seems—
> EMMA: It was the beginning of September.
> JERRY: Well, that's summer, isn't it?
> EMMA: It was actually extremely cold. It was early autumn.
> JERRY: It's pretty cold now.

As in *Old Times* (and in this respect *Betrayal* is, as Emma says, "Just like old times,") the past is what these characters need or want it to be in a present situation. Taking a good, hard look, an "objective" camera eye, the perspective Pinter has chosen to give us in *Betrayal*, will never make the same mistake, for its concern is with an entirely different level of ambiguity.

What ties this ambiguity together in the nine pieces of *Betrayal* are Pinter's images: tossing Charlotte up in the air; a tablecloth from Venice; Judith running off for a professional night shift at the ward and a romantic one with another doctor (just what was she doing lunching at Fortnum and Mason's anyway?); the references to Spinks's novel, whose subject, incidentally, is "betrayal"; the trysts and telephone calls involving Casey, the writer-client now called Roger, who has left Susannah and moved conveniently to another part of town; Jerry's lunches with Robert; the impossibility of setting a date for a game of squash; Jerry's drinking problem and his business trips to America; Emma's work at the Gallery; Ned's problem with sleeping and ours with his paternity; the schooldays back at Oxford and Cambridge with impassioned letters about Yeats and Ford Madox Ford; the trips to Venice and Yeats again on Torcello. Often involving offstage characters and specifying offstage action, these images link *Betrayal* very closely to the principle of organization Pinter used so adroitly in *The Proust Screenplay*. There Pinter shifted cinematically from one image to the next in order to highlight the wonder of a fragment which only slowly reveals itself as a small part of a far more comprehensive canvas. Proust's images, the lady in pink only later revealed as Odette, the Vermeer painting, the refrain from a Venteuil sonata, a china teacup and a silver spoon, come into focus and define themselves only through the neat pattern of incremental repetition. So it is with the images Pinter uses in *Betrayal*: characters refer to scenes we never see which then take on the materiality of actual experience. And as the characters repeat these images for us, they force us to "think back" along with them. The images accumulate and bring substance and continuity to the drama. They also make the nine scenes hold together in a dramatic unity no longer dependent for its cohesion on "real" time.

Yet *Betrayal* shows its relationship to *The Proust Screenplay* in still another important way, one which displays as well the link the play has with Pinter's work in film more generally. For in adapting *Remembrance of Things Past* to the screen, Pinter moved backward and forward in fictional time in order to visualize those effects Proust makes novelistically. And in this respect we see more precisely the primacy of that visual impact that has been at the center of Pinter's imagination in both stage and screen. After he completed the cinematic adaptation of John Fowles's *The French Lieutenant's Woman*, he was asked by one interviewer what he saw as the main difference between his work as a writer for films and for the stage:

> It's to do with certain images that you get in film you can't possibly get on the stage. A single image of Meryl Streep, for example, silent, expresses a whole volume of things . . . immediately. Now you can, of course, achieve the same kind of thing on the stage. But you have to dictate the focus by other means.

Pinter was quick to point out that in his theater the "other means" were not necessarily verbal ones:

> I don't work in purely verbal terms on the stage, by any means.
> I feel that the way an actor is sitting or standing is much to the
> point. But if there are other people on stage, you have to focus
> in quite a subtle way, actually. The discipline is very different.
> In film, you select the image.

In *Betrayal* Pinter has selected images for us by translating cinematic capabilities into what is for him a new theatrical idiom. His nine scenes of people talking allow the past to speak for itself. These may not be images for eternity, but they are without question concise momentary images of theatrical presentness. Pinter's characters are still "taking the mickey out of each other," to use Peter Hall's phrase, but his dramatic style now shows them doing it in a decidedly cinematic way. The facts of this betrayal may remain forever ambiguous, but the form in which it takes place on stage could not be more precise. Pinter has gone to the movies, but in a work like *Betrayal* he comes back, invigorated by his experience, to the theater.

THOMAS F. VAN LAAN

The Dumb Waiter: *Pinter's Play with the Audience*

Published commentary on *The Dumb Waiter* is for the most part rather unsatisfactory. Instead of analyzing the play as Pinter wrote it, most commentators rely on distortions and fabrications—or, at best, conclusions based on guesswork—to concoct a new play of their own making. The discrepancy is most apparent in the commentators' accounts of how the play ends. In the play as Pinter wrote it, after Gus has gone out the door on the left—to get a glass of water, he says—Ben hears through the speaking tube that the victim they have been waiting for "has arrived and will be coming in straight way. The normal method to be employed." Ben calls Gus, gets ready while the toilet flushes off left, calls Gus again, and then the play closes with the following stage direction.

> *The door right opens sharply.* BEN *turns, his revolver levelled at the door.*
> GUS *stumbles in.*
> *He is stripped of his jacket, waistcoat, tie, holster and revolver.*
> *He stops, body stooping, his arms at his sides.*
> *He raises his head and looks at* BEN.
> *A long silence.*
> *They stare at each other.*
> *Curtain.*

Thus Pinter. For most of the commentators, however, the play ends with the revelation that Gus is the next victim and that he is to be killed by Ben

From *Modern Drama* 24, no. 4 (December 1981). © 1981 by the University of Toronto, Graduate Centre for the Study of Drama.

because he has begun to ask too many questions rather than, like Ben, continuing blindly to obey the orders of the organizaton employing them.

There is no explicit warrant in the play for such notions, and in forming them the commentators are engaging in a process that has become widespread in the discussion of drama since the advent of Beckett. This process, which I call "filling in," is especially characteristic of commentary on Pinter—on all of his plays, not just *The Dumb Waiter*—and evidently results from the attempt to read in traditional ways a drama that has in many respects broken with traditional form. In traditional drama, the close of a play coincides with the termination of a clear-cut narrative sequence, complete with beginning, middle, and end, and culminating in an event normally of sufficient magnitude and finality to merit the label "catastrophe." This narrative sequence is, moreover, provided by the dramatist and presented to the spectators; they do not need to employ their interpretive powers to apprehend it and can therefore reserve these powers for apprehending its meaning and significance. The close of *The Dumb Waiter* does not conform to the traditional mold—there is no shot, or refusal to shoot, nor is there even any explicit indication that shooting or not shooting is at all relevant—but the commentators assume that it is meant to do so, and therefore they "fill in" what the dramatist has supposedly neglected to record except through implication. Failing to find a clear-cut narrative sequence of the sort their theatrical experience has led them to expect, they draw on their interpretive powers, not to discern meaning and significance, but to invent the missing element. They create a narrative sequence by responding imaginatively to whatever clues they can find in the text—and also, one must add, by relying heavily on the familiar patterns of melodrama.

This process is a highly questionable one. Even if we suppose that "filling in" is a legitimate activity and that the particular "filling in" provided for *The Dumb Waiter* has validity, the fact still remains that in making us determine its action before we can determine the meaning of that action, *The Dumb Waiter* differs from almost every play preceding it (and most of those coming after), and to ignore this difference is to discount a definite part of our experience and an indicator of its meaning. There is, moreover, no convincing reason to suppose that "filling in" does have legitimacy; indeed, as far as *The Dumb Waiter* is concerned, the evidence points in the other direction.

This evidence is provided by the sequence of three occasions during which Ben calls attention to an item in his newspaper, and he and Gus then subject it to a number of appropriate clichéd responses. On the first occasion, Ben reports that an eighty-seven-year-old man wanted to cross a crowded road but found the traffic too heavy to squeeze through, and so he crawled under a lorry, which then started up and ran over him. These are the responses of the two men:

GUS: Go on!
BEN: That's what it says here.
GUS: Get away.
BEN: It's enough to make you want to puke, isn't it?
GUS: Who advised him to do a thing like that?
BEN: A man of eighty-seven crawling under a lorry!
GUS: It's unbelievable.
BEN: It's down here in black and white.
GUS: Incredible.

Moments later comes the second occasion, which sounds like the first except for a crucial variation:

BEN: A child of eight killed a cat!
GUS: Get away.
BEN: It's a fact. What about that, eh? A child of eight killing a cat!
GUS: How did he do it?
BEN: It was a girl.
GUS: How did she do it?
BEN: She—
   He picks up the paper and studies it.
   It doesn't say.
GUS: Why not?
BEN: Wait a minute. It just says—her brother, aged eleven, viewed the incident from the toolshed.
GUS: Go on!
BEN: That's bloody ridiculous.
   Pause.
GUS: I bet he did it.
BEN: Who?
GUS: The brother.
BEN: I think you're right.
   Pause.
   (*Slamming down the paper.*) What about that, eh? A kid of eleven killing a cat and blaming it on his little sister of eight? It's enough to—
   He breaks off in disgust and seizes the paper.

On this occasion, Ben and Gus do not merely register the "meaning" of the news item; dissatisfied with the event given by the paper, which evidently does not conform to their notions about eight-year-old girls, they rework the data into a new event of their own making. What should be noticed especially here is the same kind of leaping to conclusions and the same air of absolute confidence in the rightness of these conclusions that characterize commentators on the play. Pinter is using Ben and Gus to mirror his audience. In this episode he creates a burlesque version of the commentators, a built-in before-the-fact put-down of their similar act of "filling in" in order to make a presented situation conform to the sense of reality the viewer has brought to it.

The third and final occasion in this sequence carries the put-down to its ultimate stage, for this time no item from the paper is actually given:

> BEN: Kaw!
>> *He picks up the paper and looks at it.*
>> Listen to this!
>> *Pause.*
>> What about that, eh?
>> *Pause.*
>> Kaw!
>> *Pause.*
>> Have you ever heard such a thing?
> GUS: (*dully*) Go on!
> BEN: It's true.
> GUS: Get away.
> BEN: It's down here in black and white.
> GUS: (*very low*) Is that a fact?
> BEN: It's enough to make you want to puke, isn't it?
> GUS: (*almost inaudible*) Incredible.

Pinter seems to be suggesting that people like Ben and Gus (and most of his commentators) scarcely need *any* objective data to inspire them when making pronouncements about the reality external to their minds, that their "responses" may not be responses at all but self-activated and self-gratifying perceptions, relying almost exclusively on internalized stereotypes.

Two commentators on *The Dumb Waiter* have managed to avoid sounding like Ben and Gus identifying the real murderer of a cat. Charles A. Carpenter has also been amused and appalled by most commentary on the play, the absurdity of which, as he shows, is by no means limited to the solemn pronouncements about Gus's being "the next victim." He properly makes fun of the typical responses, but he does not notice that Pinter himself has already done so within the play. Moreover, his own ultimate response is questionable and troublesome, for he refuses to take the play seriously. He calls it a "mock-melodramatic farce" and suggests that it is some kind of prank on Pinter's part. Thus he too tends to distort what is in actuality a profound piece of drama. Austin E. Quigley, who takes the play very seriously, has provided the best reading of it yet to appear. Quigley dismisses the typical accounts of the ending and its causes as "irrelevant speculation," preferring the more legitimate activity of trying to determine "what kinds of issues could suitably be synthesized in the lengthy . . . stare" that actually concludes the play. Quigley's careful, detailed examination of the play amply supports his view of it as a dramatization of how the odd and frightening experiences Ben and Gus are subjected to undermine their faith that the world they inhabit makes comfortable sense, that its phenomena are always familiar or at least open to ready explanation. Excellent as it is, however, Quigley's reading is not entirely satisfying. For one thing, he too is led to considerable explanation of what the characters are going through during their final stare, and while what he has to say is far subtler than the usual thing, it nonetheless borders upon "filling in." A far more important difficulty is that Quigley's article on *The Dumb Waiter*, like his brilliant and indispensable book, *The Pinter Problem*, may very well make a bit too much sense. Through his readings of Pinter, Quigley provides us with a lens for viewing the plays which frees us from having to endure the kind of experience that Ben and Gus go through and that so many spectators of Pinter's plays have felt themselves going through. In the case of *The Dumb Waiter*, by clarifying the real action of the play as thoroughly as he does and by ignoring some of its more refractory elements, Quigley domesticates it almost as effectively as do those who turn it into familiar melodrama.

It is my view that we can get most from *The Dumb Waiter* neither by denying it seriousness because of its atypical qualities nor by domesticating it in some way that lets us defuse and thus ignore its atypical qualities. We are likely, I believe, to get much closer to what Pinter is up to if we confront and try to deal with the kinds of phenomena I am concerned with here— namely, the commentators' tendency to help Pinter in his plotting, his before-the-fact mockery of this, and—something that must now be acknowledged— his clear encouragement of the very thing he mocks. The third occasion in the newspaper sequence is instructive because it employs not just one variation—the absence of an actual new item—but two. This time, although Gus says pretty much the same things, he responds *"dully,"* *"very low,"* and *"almost inaudibl[y]."* As experienced spectators, we have been trained to catch such variations and to try to figure out what has caused them. In this case, we are likely to assume that Gus's changed tone is a result of what has happened to him in this room, especially the highly disconcerting experience of the dumb waiter with its powerful suggestions that someone is unjustly tormenting him and Ben. Pinter, in other words, is in this episode clearly encouraging us to perform the same kind of activity he is simultaneously mocking. One reason, no doubt, for the commentators' excesses is encouragement of the sort Pinter offers both here and elsewhere in the play. But in responding to the encouragement while ignoring the mockery and remaining unconscious of the undue lengths to which they let the encouragement propel them, the commentators not only distort the balance in the play between encouragement and mockery, but also, in my view, overlook the real focus of the play's energies. *The Dumb Waiter*, to my mind, is as much "about" the relationship the dramatist has chosen to have with his audience as it is about anything else. And the best way to describe that relationship, as it is defined not only by the third episode with the newspaper but also by the play as a whole, is to say that with one hand Pinter beckons us to speculate while with the other he disciplines us for so doing.

All dramatists establish some kind of relationship with their spectators, but as long as it is the traditional—and comfortable—one in which the dramatist serves us as trustworthy and unobtrusive presenter of the material, we are not likely to notice the relationship as part of our experience of the play. In *The Dumb Waiter*, Pinter deviates so strikingly from the traditional model that his relationship to us becomes a central element of the drama, and if we are to understand it we are obligated to try to account for the kind of relationship he has chosen. One way of accounting is to recognize that by keeping us disoriented with regard to the proper rules for spectator response, Pinter forces us to experience much the same kind of things as Ben and Gus. But another explanation is of far greater potential interest, for it helps identify Pinter as a dramatist who is *exploring* his medium rather than merely exploiting it.

Unlike the traditional dramatist, who is concerned primarily with making meaningful events, Pinter seems far more interested in examining the process by which meaningful events are made. When *The Dumb Waiter* works the way it is supposed to, when we catch ourselves being mocked for responses it encourages us to make, we necessarily become far more conscious of our responses as such and of ourselves as responding beings than is normally the case when we are watching a play. By prompting us simultaneously to make guesses about what is happening in the play and to question ourselves self-consciously for doing so, Pinter asks us to focus not only on the play but also on ourselves, and to perceive ourselves not as passive attenders to a meaningful event shaped for us by another, but as quite uneasy collaborators with the dramatist, striving against difficulties and probably in vain to complete something that cannot fully exist without our participation. In this way, *The Dumb Waiter* serves as a commentary of sorts on our role as spectators while watching any play: it helps us to become conscious of the extent to which, by making connections to various kinds, we always contribute to the shaping of the meaningful events presented to us in the theater.

But since Pinter prompts us to reflect on our contributions to shaping his play's *action* rather than to discerning the *meaning* of that action, his manipulation of the audience in *The Dumb Waiter* is even more far-reaching in its ramifications than I have already suggested. It calls into question the conventions of traditional drama and the familiar assumptions about reality upon which these conventions are based. The traditional dramatist's presentation of a coherent action for us to interpret by making appropriate connections stems from and lends support to the popular assumption that a phenomenon such as an event exists objectively, independent of the consciousness that apprehends it, and that the proper role of this consciousness in relation to such a phenomenon is to perceive it and, where necessary, to interpret its significance by the appropriate means—usually, the laws of reason. Pinter's manipulation of us in *The Dumb Waiter* asks us to question the validity of the traditional conventions of action in drama, but he probably does this only in passing, for he seems to be after bigger game. Although we tend to respond to drama on the basis of what we have learned from our past exposure to drama—and other literary forms—we probably think of ourselves as responding to it as we respond to life outside the theater. Pinter is thus prompting us to review our assumptions about reality, to ask whether events themselves actually exist independently of our consciousness, our supposed response to them, or whether, on the contrary, our consciousness, instead of merely interpreting events, does not in fact also create them. *The Dumb Waiter* seems to ask, does an event acquire only its meaning from the way we connect data, or does it also acquire, through this process, its very existence? As Pinter has said elsewhere, "The most we know for sure is that the things which have happened have happened in a certain order: any connections we think we see, or choose to make, are pure guesswork.

If my conclusions about *The Dumb Waiter* have merit, the play offers several lessons for the reading of Pinter's work as a whole. The first and most obvious is that, whatever legitimacy "filling in" may have elsewhere—and its legitimacy for any dramatist remains undemonstrated—it is for Pinter at best a very risky process. To decide that Gus is the next victim, or that

Mick is troubled by his brother Aston's evident inability to get hold of himself, or that Ruth used to be a whore before marrying Teddy may be extremely tempting, but conclusions of this sort put too much weight on inference; they tend to eliminate the uncertainty of detail and response which is a valid element of a Pinter play, and they distract our attention from what Pinter has actually put into the play toward what we think we find there. Pinter is not trying—and failing—to create a coherent action of the traditional sort; he is creating something new and different. Instead of drawing on the traditional model in order to complete his plotting for him we should merely remain aware of this model in order to discern exactly when and how he deviates from it.

The atypical qualities of Pinter's plays—such as the bizarre behavior of the dumb waiter, or Mick's surrealistic speeches, or the non-transition-like transitions of *The Homecoming*—are not meant to be ignored or discounted as aspects of manner rather than matter. Nor are they to be argued away. Pinter is not a naturalist, as so many of his commentators wish to make him; he is, rather, a dramatist who mixes naturalism and stylization so that the seams may show and, to change metaphors, one manner clash with another. The continual occurrence of things happening or being said which defy our expectations about life and/or drama, the dizzying dislocations in which a stylistic mode that we have grown comfortable with abruptly gives way to a strikingly different one—these and similar effects are of the very essence of Pinter's drama. They are what corresponds in his plays to the coherent action that the traditional dramatist offers for our contemplation. And therefore these effects—and not some action that we have ourselves invented—constitute the proper focus of our interpretive powers and appropriately engage our efforts to discern meaning and significance.

One very important significance of these effects pertains to Pinter's handling of the relationship between the dramatist and his audience. Through the atypical qualities of his plays, Pinter tries to keep us disoriented so that we can remain aware of our own mental and emotional processes, of our involvement in the play and its making. This preoccupation of Pinter's reflects his deep interest, not only in *The Dumb Waiter* but elsewhere, in the question of how events, in drama or life, are defined. Near the end of *The Caretaker*—to cite one additional example of this interest—a faint smile exchanged between Mick and Aston encourages us to revise our entire conception of what is happening in the play. Before this smile—despite Pinter's refusal to let us get fully comfortable with the situation or the artifact dramatizing it—we had generally come to think of the action as being about Davies, about his efforts to maintain his beachhead in Aston's room notwithstanding the odds posed against him by the peculiarities of the two brothers and his own antisocial characteristics. But the smile, by suggesting some kind of conspiratorial link between the two brothers, encourages us both to infer that the action really centers on them, and to see it, in the terms of Robert P. Murphy, as "a cruel game, a game consciously and maliciously played on [Davies] . . . by both Aston and Mick." Yet the revelation is too stunning to be entirely convincing, and Pinter steadfastly refuses to confirm or deny the validity of the new view. As a result, we properly leave *The Caretaker* with two different, discordant conceptions of its action. In keeping with our usual role as spectators at a Pinter drama, we have become a part of his play. He has, in other words, been playing with us and playing us in order to make sure that our responses get called into play and into *the* play—that they become not just passive adjuncts to the dramatic experience but active and indispensable elements of its total design.

ELIN DIAMOND

Parody Play in Pinter

"Parody," Eric Bentley has said, "is more important to modern than to any previous school of comedy." Although Pinter's first critics felt his comic edge, no one before Andrew Kennedy discussed his talents for parody. Perhaps early emphasis on Pinter's originality seemed inconsistent with a form that places a writer in direct communication with predecessors and peers. Perhaps Pinter's own insistence on the spontaneity of his creative process ("I write in a very high state of excitement and frustration, I follow what I see on the paper in front of me—one sentence after another") precluded, or seemed to preclude, the idea of his using other literary and theatrical styles as targets. Pinter once declared: "I'm not interested in the general context of the theatre."

Yet Pinter the playwright was reared in the general context of the theatre. He wrote poetry while acting professionally in the companies of Anew McMaster and Sir Donald Wolfit. In 1954, under the stage name of David Baron, he toured the provinces performing popular, often stale West End fare, turning out his first drama, *The Room*, between rehearsing for one play and performing another. Later, "I finished *The Birthday Party* while I was touring in some kind of farce, I don't remember the name." In an early conversation with Richard Findlater, Pinter suggested, "my experience as an actor has influenced my plays—it must have—though it's impossible for me to put my finger on it exactly. Leslie Smith has put her finger on at least one direct influence, and Peter Davison has demonstrated links between

From *Modern Drama* 25, no. 4 (December 1982). © 1982 by University of Toronto, Graduate Centre for the Study of Drama.

music-hall rhythms and Pinter's dialogue. According to Peter Hall, the much discussed living-room set in *The Homecoming* was inspired by the broad-aproned Aldwych, where the play began its London run. Thus Pinter's artistic life thrives in a dialectical tension between what he calls "the large public activity" of theatrical production (and this includes production for radio, television and film) and the "completely private activity" of writing.

Just such a dialectic informs parody—the tension between the public domain of literary and theatrical styles, and the playwright inevitably in contact with them. Although recent studies identify parody with comically skewed imitation of an author's style or of a particular work, they stress the historical moment of the parodist who ironically plays with and criticizes a tradition even as he establishes himself within it. Bentley's reference to parody as an influential school of comedy refers to Shaw's parodies of Scribe, "[his] way of calling attention to dangerous fallacies." The "Scribe . . . counter-Scribe" in Shaw is the impulse to debunk a Scribean device by parodying it: "The very fact that Shaw despised Scribe helps to explain the particular use he made of him." In Harold Bloom's theory of poetry, "late-comer" poets make use of influential predecessors by necessarily misreading them "so as to clear imaginative space for themselves." The Russian Formalist concept of "laying bare" or using a device "without the motivation which traditionally accompanies it," is the cornerstone of Bertel Pedersen's study of parody in modern fiction; the parodist exposes "mockingly and playfully" the conventions of a genre in order to define and liberate his own creation. Kennedy (also in connection with Shaw) defines parody as the "mimesis of distorting mirrors," a concept echoed in Margaret Rose's densely theoretical work on metafictional parody: "parody does not attempt to mystify the difference between sign and signified, or to suggest an identity between itself and its object as in the mimetic art which parody has so often been used to criticise." In other words since parody is not a mirror of nature but a delib-erately skewed imitation of another representation, it lays bare the convention of mimesis, exposing it as a device. Stated or implied in these studies are four ideas relevant to parody in Pinter. First, the parodist belongs to the "endphase" of a tradition. Second, in response to that endphase he exposes and playfully recasts the conventions that inform it. Third, parodists fre-quently target the conventions of naively mimetic art. Fourth, the parodist's enterprise is inevitably self-reflexive, for in exposing the limitations of his models he comments on the form of his own creation.

Undeniably Pinter knew to his marrow the endphase of British theatre in the fifties. He memorized the lines and re-created the gestures of the well-made play style that Shaw attacked but could not kill, the style of Maugham,

Priestly, Rattigan and many others, dramatists whose work still bears revival but who rely on conventional moral attitudes, stock types, and naturalistic dialogue. Pinter has called himself a "traditional" dramatist (liking curtain lines and the suspense they provoke), but in his address to the 1962 National Student Drama festival in Bristol—a speech that reads like a parodist's manifesto—he declared war on tradition. In attacking moralizing, polemical dramatists, he implicitly attacks naively mimetic art that uses the stage to mirror conventional social hierarchies; and he prepares us for the "quicksand" experience of reality that afflicts his Rose (*The Room*), Stanley (*The Birthday Party*), Gus (*The Dumb Waiter*), and Edward (*A Slight Ache*). When he attacks contrived endings, he prepares us for his own revised "resolutions," the ambiguous tableaux on which his curtains close. When he decries character labeling and insists that his own characters tell him so much and no more, he divorces himself from those well-educated, blandly articulate types forever lighting cigarettes, pouring drinks, and gliding in and out of drawing rooms. Such familiar gestures in Pinter's play (especially in *Old Times* and *No Man's Land*) are laid bare as empty conventional signifiers, for the contexts in which they appear are anything but conventional. Finally when Pinter reacts with "nausea" to the "stale dead terminology" of our popular culture, he may be lambasting the naturalistic language of traditional drama in which predictable verbal formulas are used to reveal character relationships.

> But if it is possible to confront this nausea, to follow it to its hilt, to move through it and out of it, then it is possible to say that something has occurred, that something has been achieved.
>
> "Writing for the Theatre"

What is achieved when a writer follows a dead language to its hilt is parody, as in the conversational gambits of Spooner and Hirst, the sendup of technical jargon in the revue sketch *Trouble in the Works*. When an artist moves through and out of outmoded verbal and theatrical styles, he admits a dialogue with his precursors and then demonstrates (playfully and ironically in Pinter's case) his differences.

We can identify parodic brushstrokes throughout the Pinter canon: gangster film parody in *The Dumb Waiter*; comedy of manners parody in *The Lover* and *Betrayal*; drawing-room comedy parody in *A Slight Ache* and *No Man's Land*. However, a more complete understanding of Pinter's parodic method may be obtained by looking closely at one play, *The Collection*, a work not normally considered to be parodic. Written for television in 1961, *The Collection* involves four West End fashion designers, James and Stella, Harry and Bill, whose lives intertwine when James seeks the truth about Stella's confessed adultery with Bill at a dress collection showing in Leeds. During the play five different versions of the adultery emerge, including the possibility that it never happened. Because everyone lies at some point during the play, the truth about the incident becomes splintered into a series of subjective truths based on personal and unknowable motives. According to the playwright:

> When an event occurs—some kind of sexual event in *The Collection*, for example—it is made up of many little events. Each person will take away and remember what is most significant to him. The more other people try to verify the less they know.

But the less they know the more they speculate, creating an atmosphere of anxious uncertainty.

The Collection parodies two related popular dramatic styles, nineteenth-century domestic melodrama and television soap opera. That is, Pinter parodies the melodramatic plot conventions in which past sins create emotional chaos in the present and the soap-opera convention of the unending problem, unraveling in an atmosphere of unanswered questions, stammering, accusations, and tears. In fact *The Collection* provides a fine test case for parody: the play's comic incongruities are purchased at the expense of the conventions, the character types, and the gloom-and-tears mood of both of these popular genres.

At first glance it seems incongruous to associate melodramas in which fallen women soliloquized passionately to tearful audiences with the bloodless soap opera enclosed in its sterile electronic box. Yet radio and television soap operas are the modern incarnations of popular domestic melodrama. Both are based on a formula of flat characters and broad coincidence; both focus on problems of love, marriage, and family; both reinforce conventional morality; and both are afflicted with a disease Robert Heilman calls "monopathy," in which emotions, like the characters themselves, are unifaceted, unqualified, to the point of being obsessional—the kind of stock representations Pinter objected to in his Drama Festival speech. In *Lost in London* and *East Lynne*, two popular melodramas of the 1860's, the protracted sufferings of fallen women dominate the action. In *East Lynne*, Isabel Archer leaves her husband and children to run off with Sir Francis Levison, who deserts her after she bears their illegitimate child. Isabel returns to East Lynne as a governess (her sin-worn face her only disguise) and after exquisite suffering finally dies, recognized and forgiven, in her husband's arms.

With the move toward social realism, fallen women were less a disease than a problem and monopathetic suffering was replaced by a more complex anxiety. Jones's *Mrs. Dane's Defence* and Pinero's *The Second Mrs. Tanqueray* both treat the subject of the woman with a past who tries to rehabilitate herself through marriage. The past catches up with Mrs. Dane in the person of Sir Daniel Carteret, a trial judge and guardian of Mrs. Dane's young fiancé. At the climax of the play, Sir Daniel cross-examines Mrs. Dane, peeling off layer upon layer of lies until he exposes her true identity. In Pinero's drama, Paula Ray's past is known to her husband, but she stands condemned by his daughter, by his own ineptitude and, most of all, by her obsessively guilty conscience: "I'm tainted through and through; anybody can see it." Pinero attempts psychological complexity by employing a device we recognize from soap opera, the nonending. Thus Paula's formulaic suicide is followed by her stepdaughter's guilty confession, and after she *"faints upon the ottoman,"* the family friend pauses *"irresolutely—then . . . goes to the door, opens it and stands looking out."* Neither in nor out of the room, he creates an impression of uncertainty and inconclusiveness.

Cliffhanger finishes are, of course, fundamental to soap opera, in which "people agonize over decisions, and worry about what the results of their actions will be. Should Barbara marry Tony when she is not sure she loves him? Should Tara . . . [identify] the father of her unborn child?" The monopathy of anxiety is made possible by the nonending and intensified by television camera techniques which bring into close range the characters' darting eyes, quivering lips, twitching and furrowed brows. Such signifiers are smaller but no more complex than the heroine wringing her hands or fainting upon the ottoman; they telegraph the obsessional anxiety that soap opera inherits from melodrama.

What about *The Collection*? No one would accuse Pinter of transparency. The instant gratifications of melodrama and soap opera are absent from Pinter's emotional spectrum. Feelings are filtered through a highly contrived arrangement of pause and silence and verbal maneuvering. As opposed to the verbosity of suffering in soap opera, "the more acute the experience" in a Pinter work, "the less articulate its expression." In *The Collection*, however, action arises out of a banal incident suggestive of conventional anxiety and tears: Stella's apparent adultery with Bill. In a typical Victorian melodrama, Stella would suffer hideous remorse, James would suffer rage mingled with heartbreak, a suffering Harry would intercede with the couple, and the insufferable Bill would melt from his posture of cold uncaring. At least one of the four would die of grief. The soap-opera version would be less exciting, as the writer would endeavor to extend the aftermath of Leeds for at least a month, return to it constantly for three months, then intermittently for the next six to eight months.

Essential to the humor of *The Collection* is Pinter's parody of the sin-suffering dynamic, a parody we appreciate best by noting his use and abuse of conventions. *The Collection* contains an unusual number of typical melodramatic signifiers. For example, James's recriminations provoke real tears from Stella, reminiscent of tormented fallen women:

> I don't know what you're . . . I just don't know what you're . . .
> I just . . . hoped you'd understand . . .
> *She covers her face, crying.*

As the melodramatic villain was identified by black clothing and wig, Stella is identified with her white kitten, suggesting a feline seductress who guards claws under a guise of softness and fragility. Music, another traditional labeling device, provides commentary on both Stella and Bill. When Stella puts on a Charlie Parker record in her darkened apartment, then lies back on the sofa stroking the kitten, she creates an impression of both loneliness and sexual readiness. Vivaldi as background music shows Bill's desire to appear refined, but the transistor radio suggests his transitory position in Harry's house. Name labels, a device as old as the morality play and rampant in Victorian melodrama, ironically gloss the personalities of three of the characters. Harry's surname, "Kane," puns on the Biblical Cain, who asks, "Am I my brother's keeper?" Harry "keeps" Bill economically and sexually, and also canes him verbally at the end of the play. James Horne is "horned" or cuckolded by his wife's adultery and reacts by horning in on the private lives of Harry and Bill. Stella, not quite a fixed star, illuminates nothing and appears unreachable at the play's conclusion.

The setting of *The Collection* offers up other familiar signifiers. Conceived initially for television, the scenic directions point to the kind of sketched-in realism and class-labeling we associate with television soap opera. Harry's Belgravia house has "Elegant décor. Period furnishing"; James's Chelsea flat has "tasteful contemporary furnishing." The prominent position of the telephone booth ("Upstage centre on promontory") sketches in the street and our modern world of electronic communication. Moreover, the opening action of the play plunges us into a mood of mystery and soap-opera anxiety. A "*figure . . . dimly observed*" enters the telephone booth and calls Harry, but maliciously refuses to identify himself. Even in the printed text, Pinter conceals his identity, "Voice" concluding the conversation with an ominous "Tell him I'll be in touch." Pinter supplements verbal mystery with a visual tableau. Harry stands still, radiating perplexity, suspicion, perhaps fear. On television the camera naturally closes in, combing the actor's face, inviting us to wonder less about the characters of the two men than about what the call means. In the best tradition of soap opera we are instantly launched into the action, anticipating more information.

Immediately following, the first scene with James and Stella is tour-de-force imitation of monopathetic soap-opera tension. Stella is about to leave for the shop as James sits on the sofa smoking. In reaction to her simple yet resonating question, "What are you going to do?," James "*looks at her, with a brief smile, then away.*" His silence causes her to stammer:

> Jimmy . . .
> *Pause.*
> Are you going out?
> *Pause.*
> Will you . . . be in tonight?

In response "JAMES *reaches for a glass ashtray, flicks ash, and regards the ashtray.* STELLA *turns and leaves the room. The front door slams.* JAMES *continues regarding the ashtray.*" The characters know more than we do, but the situation is fraught with so many familiar soap-opera signals—the ash flicked, the door slammed, the tableau of the lone figure fixing his gaze on anything but the cause of his tension—that we feel at least superficially informed. This is marital tension in the soap-opera world. We know there will be a sequel.

Yet the metaphysical implications of the sequel are subverted in Pinter's parody. Fundamental to the plots of domestic melodrama and soap opera is the verifiability of the past. The sins of Isabel Archer, Mrs. Dane, and Paula Tanqueray must be real in order to justify their long and instructive suffering. What leads James to Bill and back to Stella is the belief that the truth lies buried in the past and that if it were known the incident itself could be purged. James discovers, of course, that the past is not only uncertain but unknowable. Parodying the moral logic of fallen-women melodramas in which sinners stand confronted by their sins, *The Collection* explores the existential logic of uncertainty. The past twists and turns in on itself. As the play progresses in time, James moves back in knowledge, sure of less at the end than at the beginning.

Sequential logic in soap operas and melodramas hinges on the rhetoric of the question. Correctly posed questions yield answers that establish facts and become truths. Pinter parodies the interrogation process in *The Birthday Party* and *No Man's Land*, using questions not to elicit answers but to intimidate and victimize characters. In *The Collection* interrogations are subtler, as fact-finding becomes a game of comic evasion. Having drawn the cuckold's card, James taunts Stella either by refusing to answer her questions (in their first exchange) or by asking her questions to which there can be no right answer. "What is your aim?"; "You know what you've got?" With Bill the game is more entertaining, for unlike Stella, Bill is an apt and intriguing opponent. His first move is to refuse to be interrogated, leaving the house before James arrives. Once caught, he adopts at once James's tactic of parrying questions with questions:

JAMES: Got any olives?
BILL: How did you know my name?

Then, when James, like Sir Daniel in *Mrs. Dane's Defence*, launches a careful cross-examination, Bill converts the interrogation into witty banter:

JAMES: You booked into 142. But you didn't stay there.
BILL: Well, that's a bit silly, isn't it? Booking a room and not staying in it?
JAMES: 165 is just along the passage to 142; you're not far away.
BILL: Oh well, that's a relief.

Eventually Bill parodies James's interrogation with one of his own:

BILL: . . . Is she supposed to have resisted me at all?
JAMES: A little.
. . . .
BILL: Did she bite at all?
JAMES: No.
BILL: Scratch?
JAMES: A little.
BILL: She scratched a little did she? Where? (*Holds up a hand.*) On the hand? No scar. No scar anywhere. Absolutely unscarred. We can go before a commissioner of oaths, if you like. I'll strip, show you my unscarred body. Yes, what we need is an independent witness. You got any chambermaids on your side or anything?

Since James is obsessed with the logistics of the bedroom and the color of Bill's pajamas, Bill adds the detail of tattling chambermaids, transforming the Leeds hotel into a backdrop for a French farce. He even appropriates a traditional device from well-made plots: the telltale scar. James applauds Bill's clever performance, cuing audience laughter.

Bill's comically distorted view of the Leeds hotel is in keeping with the gamelike distortions riddling Pinter's parodic text. Adapted from television, Pinter's double set creates a double focus for the audience that undermines the mimetic validity of either world. The shifting between sets becomes less a matter of realistic visitation than a metaphor for the fast changing versions of the adultery story. Furthermore, the set provokes internal parody, scenes mirroring scenes with increasing distortion. Harry replaces James as the *"figure . . . dimly seen"* in the telephone booth, his purpose being not to probe further but to end all further probing. Harry and Stella agree that James had concocted a "fantastic story," a version which Harry himself revises by claiming that Stella alone had concocted it—another fantastic story. The verbal gamesmanship in James's first scene with Bill is echoed but deflected in a kind of parodic truth when James scars Bill's hand, thereby "proving" his own version of the story. Stella finishes the play by cruelly mimicking James's silence in their opening dialogue, her inscrutable smile contradicting her earlier tears. (Pinter tells us that her face is *"friendly, sympathetic,"* but this cannot be verified.) Finally, the fade-ups and fade-outs which open and close each mini-installment parody the picture-frame resolutions of melodrama and the cliffhanger conclusions of soap opera. Pinter's tableaux offer fleeting unstable images, and the closing image, showing two couples at stalemate, neither resolves the action nor points toward a future resolution.

The internal distortions produced by the double set and the shifting versions of the event in Leeds are enhanced by verbal play. Simon Trussler has complained that "the characters [in *The Collection*] talk not like members of the upper-middle class pretending to be classless, but like upper-middle class characters imitating people in plays." This is an astute observation, and it supports the argument for parody in the text. Pinter imitates and fractures the banal mimetic language of soap-opera confrontation. *The Collection* is packed with double-entendres, from puns on pouffes and fruit knives to Bill's ironical "I'm going to be Minister for Home Affairs." As is typical with Pinter, repetition in phatic interchanges produces an ironic pattern. Although the characters perpetuate deceit, they parrot clarity:

> JAMES: . . . I can see it both ways, three ways, all ways . . .
> every way. It's perfectly clear. . . .

> HARRY: It's all quite clear now.
> STELLA: I'm glad.

> JAMES: Well, thanks very much, Mr. Kane, for clearing my
> mind.

Such clarities are ironic refractions, images of each person's distortion of the incident at Leeds.

Verbal refractions are themselves imaged in the "deceptive" mirror to which we are introduced in Bill's second scene with James. Mirroring reality, mimetic art presents us with characters, action, and dialogue corresponding to the behavior and speech of recognizable people. But the characters in *The Collection* are deliberately truncated, impossible to identify with. The double set and the constant play of lights break emotional continuity by heightening our awareness of theatrical devices at work. These fashion designers move like mannequins, set up and controlled by their maker. Similarly, while dialogue reflects familiar emotional anxieties, the play's language contains the comic potential to mock those anxieties. And the adultery itself, an event that would usually launch a series of predictable reactions, subtly transforms into a metaphor for metaphysical uncertainty.

Through James, Pinter lays bare the mimetic assumptions underlying domestic melodrama and soap opera. Like a conventional moralist, James believes that the truth is knowable and will out eventually. He fails to see that the mirror might be deceptive, just as he fails to see that artifical re-productions of reality (the fictions of Bill and Stella) have nothing to do with the actual experience of reality. James is both a monopathetic sufferer and a throwback to naive realism. In Pinter's parodic reworking of melodrama and soap opera, he is also a comic butt.

The Collection works at another level of comedy, the audience's recognition of references to art and to Pinter's art within the play. The stage imagery and internal parody of *The Collection* anticipate the self-reflexive features in Pinter's work of the seventies. In *Old Times*, Anna is both present and not present at the opening; in *No Man's Land*, Foster seems to extinguish the theatre lights as well as the lights to the stage room; and in *Betrayal*, time twists backward and forward—in these instances Pinter comments on the theatrical conventions of realism which dictate that characters on stage must be assumed to hear one another, that an anonymous technician controls the stage lights, and that time will proceed with linear regularity. The fore-grounding of Pinter's own conventions—the themes of menacing intrusion and unverifiability—which occurs in these later plays is evident in *The Collection* as well. Bill's lines to James, "You're not my guest, you're an intruder. What can I do for you?", evoke the dangerous intruders of Pinter's early plays and mockingly neutralize the reference in repartee. James's line to Stella, "He [Bill] entirely confirmed your story," reuses Pinter's impossibility-of-verification theme in a context of ironic prevarication. And Bill, the worst liar in the play, is allowed to mouth Pinter's greatest untruth:

> Surely the wound heals when you know the truth, doesn't it? I mean, when the truth is verified? I would have thought it did.

With James's reference to the mirror, self-parody dovetails into self-reflexiveness; that is, Pinter's own philosophy of experience conflates with the laying bare of mimetic conventions. From this perspective, the "deceptive" mirror may be not a subtle "slip," as one critic has suggested, but rather the playwright's cue to his audience and his critics to take note of the author's game-playing as well as the character's game-playing in the text.

Any discussion of parody or self-parody must include consideration of audience response, for parody assumes that a work is perceived not in isolation but rather as a comically skewed imitation of specific literary and theatrical styles. I am not suggesting that an audience at *The Collection* will consciously perceive the conventions of melodrama and soap opera or that Pinter had them specifically in mind when he wrote the play. I *am* suggesting that we, like Pinter, are inevitably attuned to the stale conventions of popular forms, and that the comic incongruities in *The Collection* and other plays derive, in part, from Pinter's ingenious and parodic manipulation of those conventions.

In a recent article, Thomas Van Laan cautioned critics to acknowledge fully the "dizzying dislocations" in a Pinter text instead of trying to "fill in" or to explain them away. My argument for parody takes a similar point of view. It proposes that criticism of Pinter's comedy take into consideration the complex intersections of at least two areas of experience: the conventions of precursor styles, and the ways in which Pinter attacks and revises those conventions in his plays. To view Pinter as a parodist is to appreciate his own (somewhat ironic) self-estimation as a "traditional" writer. Pinter is a traditional writer in that he carefully and comically works "through . . . and out of" tradition, constructing new art from the dying devices of the old.

MARTIN ESSLIN

Language and Silence

That Pinter has added a new band of colours to the spectrum of English stage dialogue is attested by the frequent use of terms like "Pinteresque language" or "Pinterese" in current dramatic criticism. Some of the more obvious features of his use of language, such as recurrent tautologies on the pattern "He's old—Not young—No, I wouldn't call him young—Not youthful, certainly—Elderly, I'd say—I'd call him old" have been copied to the point of parody by a large number of aspiring authors. And the bad imitations have, inevitably, cast a shadow over the original user—and indeed, discoverer, of these linguistic absurdities which had hitherto largely escaped the attentive ears of playwrights. Yet these most easily recognizable features of Pinter's dialogue are, on the whole, the most superficial aspects of his artistry; moreover, even their function in the overall picture has been largely misunderstood, for while Pinter undoubtedly *has* an uncannily accurate ear for the linguistic solecisms of the English vernacular spoken by ordinary people, it is neither his special intention or foremost dramatic purpose merely to amuse his audience by confronting them with accurately observed examples of linguistic nonsense and thus giving them the pleasure of *recognizing* the linguistic mistakes of others and feeling superior to them. It may be true that a good deal of Pinter's initial success was, indeed, perhaps due to this kind of audience reaction, and he may even, occasionally, have succumbed to the temptation of exploiting it; yet, if his work is seen as a whole it will be recognized that he has also resisted this temptation—and with considerable

From *Pinter the Playwright*. © 1970, 1973, 1977, 1982 by Martin Esslin. Methuen and Co., Ltd., 1970.

success—not only by at first discarding plays like *The Hothouse* (which might have been regarded at the time as an overindulgence in Pinterese), but also by moving out of the sphere of low-life dialogue in the plays which followed the success of *The Caretaker* (*The Lover*, *The Collection*, and later *Tea Party* and *The Basement*); by avoiding the tricks of the more obvious Pinterese in a play which might well have given a great deal of opportunity for self-copying and self-parody—*The Homecoming*; and, finally, by abandoning naturalistic action and dialogue altogether in the next phase of his development—the highly compressed stage poetry of recollected experience in *Landscape*, *Silence*, *Old Times*, *Betrayal*, and *A Kind of Alaska*.

A true understanding of Pinter's use of language must, I believe, be based on deeper, more fundamental considerations: it must start from an examination of the function of language in stage dialogue generally—and indeed from considerations of the use of language in ordinary human intercourse itself. For here—at least as far as the English language is concerned—Pinter has given us added insight into—has, in a certain measure even *discovered*—the fact that traditional stage dialogue has always greatly overestimated the degree of logic which governs the use of language, the amount of information which language is actually able to impart on the stage—as in life. People on the stage have, from Sophocles to Shakespeare to Rattigan, always spoken more clearly, more directly, more to the purpose than they would ever have done in real life. This is obvious enough in verse drama which had to obey not only the rules of prosody, but also those of the ancient art of rhetoric, which concerned itself with the ways in which speech could be made as clear, well proportioned and eaily assimilated as possible. So strong was this tradition that it even persisted in naturalistic drama although it was sometimes superficially disguised; the finest speeches in Ibsen or Shaw are as brilliantly constructed as those of Cicero or Demosthenes. And even in the scenes of light conversation in the exposition of these plays the main emphasis lies on the elegance with which the essential *information* about the antecedents of the plot and the motivation of the characters is conveyed, broken up perhaps into seemingly casually arranged fragments, but nevertheless in a discursive, explicit style.

It was only gradually that a certain defectiveness of communication between characters—who talk past each other rather than to each other—was introduced by dramatists like Strindberg or Wedekind; and that "oblique" dialogue in which the text hints at a hidden subtext was brought in by Chekhov; as in the climactic scene of *The Cherry Orchard* discussed in an earlier chapter of this book, when the real action—Lopakhin's failure to declare himself to Varya—is taking place beneath a trivial exchange about a missing article of clothing. But this scene was elaborately *prepared* by Chekhov: he had taken care in the preceding scene to make it quite explicit to the audience that they were to expect Lopakhin's offer of marriage. Pinter's technique continues Chekhov's use of such "oblique" dialogue, but carries it much further.

A comparison between two climactic closing scenes by the two playwrights might serve to illustrate this point:

In the closing scene of Chekhov's *Uncle Vanya* the chief characters have lost their hope of love and fulfilment. Vanya turns to Sonia and expresses his feelings in a highly explicit outburst:

> My child, there's such a weight on my heart! Oh, if only you knew how my heart aches.

And Sonia replies:

> Well, what can we do? We must go on living! (*A pause.*) We shall go on living, Uncle Vanya. We shall live through a long, long succession of days and tedious evenings. We shall patiently suffer the trials which Fate imposes on us; we shall work for others, now and in our old age, and we shall have no rest.

Having described the reality of their lives to come, Sonia turns to talk of the remaining great hope of eternal rest—in death:

> We shall rest! We shall hear the angels, we shall see all the heavens covered with stars like diamonds, we shall see all earthly evil, all our sufferings swept away by the grace which will fill the whole world, and our life will become peaceful, gentle and sweet as a caress. I believe it, I believe it. . . . Poor, poor Uncle Vanya, you're crying. . . . You've had no joy in life, but wait, Uncle Vanya, wait . . . we shall rest . . . We shall rest. . . . we shall rest!

A magnificent piece of writing, but surely very far removed from the way in which a girl like Sonia would use language in a real situation of this kind. The rhetorical heritage is still very strong in Chekhov's style. There *is* an element of "obliqueness" present even here, however: for while Sonia professes to *believe* in the joys of eternal bliss in heaven, we know that what she is saying is *not* what she really believes; she is using the picture of heavenly bliss as a last despairing attempt at bringing consolation to Uncle Vanya. It is in the contrast between what is being said and what lies behind it that

the poignancy and also the innovatory modernity of Chekhov's approach to
language in drama appears.

Pinter, in the final scene of *The Birthday Party*, which portrays a situation
that is analogous to the close of *Uncle Vanya*—the loss of the hope of love
suffered by Meg—goes infinitely further than Chekhov. Pinter's characters
do not talk explicitly about the situation at all. Meg knows, deep down, that
Stanley has gone, but she cannot and will not admit it to herself; and Petey
is too inarticulate to offer a speech of consolation like Sonia's:

> MEG: I was the belle of the ball.
> PETEY: Were you?
> MEG: Oh yes. They all said I was.
> PETEY: I bet you were, too.
> MEG: Oh, it's true. I was.
> *Pause.*
> I know I was.

Four times Meg repeats that she was the belle of the ball—the disastrous
party through which her substitute son was destroyed and taken away from
her. It is quite clear that she does not in fact want to say anything about
the impression she actually made at that party. She is, in fact, merely trying
to hang on to the illusion that everything is still as it was, that the disastrous
party was not a disaster but the success she had hoped for it. The fourfold
repetition of the statement does not derive from any desire to say the same
thing four times; it is no more than a sign of the desperateness of her attempt,
her pitiful determination not to let the realization of the disaster dawn on
her. Hence the repetition of the statement is more relevant than the statement
and the explicit, "discursive" content of the statement, itself. Similarly
Petey's affirmation that the statement is true merely has the function of
expressing his compassion, his despair and, above all, his inability to do
anything towards making Meg acknowledge or realize the true position. Thus
the dramatic effect of this brilliantly moving, brilliantly economical and
concise passage of dialogue is entirely due to the complete contradiction
between the words that are spoken and the emotional and psychological
action which underlies them. Here the language has almost totally lost its
rhetorical, its informative element and has fully merged into dramatic action.

It is true that in a passage of dialogue like this there is little verbal
communication between the characters in that Meg does not inform Petey
of any fact she wants him to know, nor he her. Yet to sum up this state of
affairs by labelling such a passage a dialogue of noncommunication completely misses the point of the matter. For Pinter is far from wanting to say

that language is incapable of establishing true communication between human beings; he merely draws our attention to the fact that in life human beings rarely make use of language for that purpose, at least as far as spoken, as distinct from written, language is concerned. People interact not so much logically as emotionally through language; and the tone of voice, the emotional colour of the words is often far more significant than their exact meanings, by their dictionary definition; we all know that an outburst of name-calling by one person against another is basically an act of aggression, an assault by verbal blows in which the violence of the emotion behind the words is far more important than their content. Where animals use physical action and physical contact (such as sniffing each other, catching each others' fleas) human beings, through the power of speech, can substitute verbal contact and verbal action (small talk about the weather, exchange of information about one's minor ailments, abuse or words of endearment). What matters in most oral verbal contact therefore is more what people are *doing* to each other through it rather than the conceptual content of what they are saying.

Thus in drama dialogue is, ultimately, a form of *action*; it is the element of action, the interaction between the characters, their reactions to each other, which constitute the truly *dramatic* element in stage dialogue, its essential aspect in the context of drama, apart from and over and above all the other values embodied in the writing such as wit, lucidity, elegance of structure and logical development, depth of thought, persuasiveness, rhythm, imagery, mellifluousness and sheer beauty as poetry—all the rhetorical and literary qualities which could also be appreciated outside the context of drama.

But being essentially action, dramatic dialogue is not necessarily the dominant element in the playwright's armoury: it may be equally or even less important than the nonverbal actions of the characters and, indeed, their silences. Traditionally, however, because of the origins of dramatic writing in the art of oratory, dialogue has been the dominant element in drama. Hence the tendency for drama to involve highly articulate characters, the only ones who would naturally interact in terms of brilliantly phrased speech; this showed itself in the need to *stylize* the verbal expression by the use of verse, which relieved the playwright of the need to imitate the real speech of characters who in reality would have been inarticulate, or at least far from possessing the powers of expression with which they seemed to be endowed on the stage; or, in later, naturalistic drama the tendency to place the action among people who would be highly articulate in real life: the elegant wits of Wilde, the eloquent intellectuals of Shaw. Only when it was recognized that the verbal element need not be the dominant aspect of drama, or at least that it was not the content of what was said that mattered most, but the action which it embodied, and that inarticulate, incoherent, tautological and nonsensical speech might be as dramatic as verbal brilliance when it could be treated simply as an element of action, only then did it become possible to place inarticulate characters in the centre of the play and to make their unspoken emotions transparent. Pinter is among the discoverers of this highly significant aspect of drama.

If we examine some of Pinter's favourite linguistic and stylistic devices in the light of these considerations, we shall find that far from being mere verbal absurdities held up to ridicule, they do in fact illuminate the mental processes that lie behind the ill-chosen or nonsensical words; and that in each case superficially similar quirks of language may serve quite different dramatic functions.

Take the most obvious of these, the one most frequently attributed to Pinter as a mere mannerism: repetition. Each time Pinter's characters repeat themselves, or each others' phrases, the playwright employs the device of repetition to fulfil a definite function in the action; if, for example, at the beginning of *The Birthday Party* Meg, having served Petey his cornflakes, asks:

MEG: Are they nice?
PETEY: Very nice.
MEG: I thought they'd be nice.

The emptiness of the dialogue clearly indicates the emptiness of the characters' relationship with each other, the boredom of their lives and yet their determination to go on making friendly conversation. So this short dialogue of no more than ten words, three of which are repetitions of "nice," which on the surface, conveys no worthwhile *conceptual* information whatever, does in fact compress a very considerable amount of *dramatic* information—this being the exposition of the play—and dramatic action, i.e. the vain attempt at conversation, the desire to be friendly—into an astonishingly brief space.

If, on the other hand, Davies in *The Caretaker*, talking about his ex-wife's slovenliness, mentions the saucepan in which he found some of her underclothing, repeats himself, saying:

The pan for vegetables, it was. The vegetable pan,

the repetition serves a completely different purpose: it shows us this inarticulate man's struggle to find the correct word, the *mot juste*. Traditional

stage dialogue always tended to err on the side of assuming that people have
the right expression always ready to suit the occasion. In Pinter's dialogue
we can always watch the desperate struggles of his characters to find the
correct expression; we are thus enabled to see them in the—very dramatic—
act of struggling for communication, sometimes succeeding, often failing.
And when they have got hold of a formulation, they hold on to it, savour
it and repeat it to enjoy their achievement, like Gus in *The Dumb Waiter*
when he recalls the time they killed a girl:

> It was a mess though, wasn't it? What a mess. Honest, I can't
> remember a mess like that one. They don't seem to hold together
> like men, women. A looser texture, like. Didn't she spread, eh?
> She didn't half spread. Kaw!

The pleasure with which Gus dwells on the words *mess* and *spread* is evident:
not because he enjoyed killing the girl, quite the contrary; but because, being
an inarticulate person who has trouble in finding the expressive phrase, he
loves to play with and savour it once he has got hold of it and does not want
to let it go. He is delighted to have found the expressive image of the girl's
body dissolving like butter: "she spread." So, while on one level he is worried
and unhappy about his job as a killer and deplores having had to liquidate
that girl, on another he revels in the happy feeling of having expressed his
thought well. Another example of how dialogue which is primitive and crude
when judged by the standards of rhetoric, can be astonishingly subtle, ironical and psychologically penetrating if considered as an expression of character in action—drama.

As against the use of repetition to show a character's *enjoyment* at having
found the *mot juste*, there is repetition as a form of hysterical irritation: so
obsessed, for example, is McCann in *The Birthday Party* with the unpleasantness of what he and Goldberg will have to do to Stanley, that he breaks
out:

> Let's finish and go. Let's get it over and go. Get the thing done.
> Let's finish the bloody thing. Let's get the thing done and go!

McCann's hysteria emerges not only from the frantic rhythm with which
these sentences are phrased but also from the obsessive permutation of the
same elements—"finish," "go," "get done."

Conversely, Pinter uses repetition to show how a character gradually
learns to accept a fact which at first he had difficulty in taking in. Having
been terrorized by Mick, Davies in *The Caretaker* asks Aston:

DAVIES: Who was that feller?
ASTON: He's my brother.
DAVIES: Is he? He's a bit of a joker, en'he?
ASTON: Uh.
DAVIES: Yes . . . he's a real joker.
ASTON: He's got a sense of humour.
DAVIES: Yes, I noticed.
> *Pause.*
> He's a real joker, that lad, you can see that.
> *Pause.*
ASTON: Yes, he tends . . . he tends to see the funny side of things.
DAVIES: Well, he's got a sense of humour, en'he?
ASTON: Yes.
DAVIES: Yes, you could tell that.
> *Pause.*

Here the manner in which Davies takes up Aston's phrase about the "sense of humour" and the way in which he punctuates his realization of Mick's character with "I noticed," "you can see that" and "you could tell that" allows the audience to witness the slow sinking in of the facts, the gradual evaluation of the man he met, the eventual and increasingly bitter coming to terms with these facts in Davies's mind. Two repeated phrases are interlocked in this passage ("he's a joker/got a sense of humour" and "I noticed/can see/could tell that") and again their various permutations in the mouth of first the one and then the other character give the dialogue a definite poetic shape, a musical form of theme and variations, of strophe and antistrophe: psychological realism and a poet's control over the formal element in language are here fused in a way highly characteristic of Pinter.

For repetition, which, as Pinter has discovered, is an aspect of real speech that stage dialogue had neglected under the influence of the rhetorical tradition (which rejects recurrence of the same word as stylistically inelegant) is, of course, also one of the most important elements of poetry—particularly in the form of whole phrases which recur as refrains, for example in ballad metre. On the realistic level Pinter uses the refrain-like recurrence of whole sentences to show that people in real life do not deliver well thought-out set speeches but tend to mix various logical strands of thought which intermingle without any permanent connection: while the structure of rhetorical or written language tends to be logical, that of spoken language is associative. In the first act of *The Caretaker*, for example, Aston tells Davies that there is a family of Indians living in the house next door. Davies immediately reacts with:

DAVIES: Blacks?
ASTON: I don't see much of them.
DAVIES: Blacks, eh?

The conversation then turns to other matters and Davies embarks on his story about his Odyssey to the monastery at Luton where he had been told the monks handed out shoes to the poor. Having reached the climax of that story, he is about to introduce the punch line:

> You know what that bastard monk said to me?
> *Pause.*
> How many more Blacks you got around here then?
> ASTON: What?
> DAVIES: You got any more Blacks around here?

Without any *logical* motivation the question about the Blacks reemerges to the surface a minute or more after it was first mooted. But the association is clear enough: the hatred and indignation Davies feels for the monk who treated him so badly has reawakened the emotion of fear and hatred against that other archenemy of his—the coloured community.

Similarly, in Davies's long speech of hatred against Aston, when he believes that Mick will support him in giving him control of the house and he tries to assert his superiority over Aston, as a former inmate of a mental institution, we find several lines of thought mixed to give a refrain-like effect:

> I'm a sane man! So don't start mucking me about. I'll be all right as long as you keep your place. Just you keep your place, that's all. *Because I can tell you, your brother's got his eye on you.* He knows all about you. I got a friend there, don't you worry about that. I got a true pal there. Treating me like dirt! Why'd you invite me in here in the first place if you was going to treat me like this? You think you're better than me you got another think coming. I know enough. They had you inside one of them places before, they can have you inside again. *Your brother's got his eye on you!* They can put the pincers on your head again, man. [My italics]

It is clear that this type of associative structure in which several basic thoughts (I am better than you because I am sane, you have been in a mental insti-tution—your brother is my friend, he has his eye on you) intermingle in ever recurring variations belongs on the whole to characters of Davies's primitive mentality. But Pinter also uses it, in an appropriately modified form, in the mouth of one of his most sophisticated characters, Harry, the rich clothing manufacturer in *The Collection*:

> Bill's a slum boy, you see, he's got a slum sense of humour. That's why I never take him along with me to parties. Because he's got a slum mind. I have nothing against slum minds *per se*, you understand, nothing at all. There's a certain kind of slum mind which is perfectly all right in a slum, but when this kind of slum mind gets out of the slum it sometimes persists, you see, it rots everything. That's what Bill is. There's something faintly putrid about him, don't you find? Like a slug. There's nothing wrong with slugs in their place, but he's a slum slug; there's nothing wrong with slum slugs in their place, but this one won't keep his place—he crawls all over the walls of nice houses, leaving slime, don't you, boy? He confirms stupid sordid little stories just to amuse himself, while everyone else has to run round in circles to get to the root of the matter and smooth the whole thing out. All he can do is sit and suck his bloody hand and decompose like the filthy putrid slum slug he is.

Here the structure is apparently one of rigid logic, even of syllogism, but only apparently. For the real motivation for the erection of this structure of pseudologic is to give an opportunity to hammer away at the humiliating terms *slum* and *slug*; the repetition here indicates the degree of Harry's obsession with Bill and his hatred of him, but it is also deliberately used by him as a means of aggression, of mental torture and humiliation towards Bill. And again the refrain-like recurrence of the same type of phrase (I have nothing against, There is nothing wrong) gives this highly realistic and closely observed reproduction of genuine speech patterns a musical-poetic structure.

In Harry's diatribe the emotional charge of jealousy, hatred and contempt underlies the associative structure of his speech. In other instances it is, on the other hand, the absence of emotion, the determination to avoid saying what ought to be said, that leads to associative and equally repetitious sequences of words. When Davies, in *The Caretaker*, first encounters Mick, is frightened by him and asks who he is, Mick, who wants to torment him by keeping him on tenterhooks, embarks on a long diatribe which is quite obviously intended to convey no information whatever:

> You know, believe it or not, you've got a funny kind of resemblance to a bloke I once knew in Shoreditch. Actually he lived

in Aldgate. I was staying with a cousin in Camden Town. This
chap, he used to have a pitch in Finsbury Park, just by the bus
depot. When I got to know him I found out he was brought up
in Putney. That didn't make any difference to me. I know quite
a few people who were born in Putney. Even if they weren't born
in Putney, they were born in Fulham. The only trouble was, he
wasn't born in Putney, he was only brought up in Putney. It
turned out he was born in the Caledonian Road, just before you
get to the Nag's Head.

Not only is this passage, in its total nonsensicality, highly comic, not only
does it prolong Davies's and the audience's suspense, it also shows the thought
process which prompts Mick: one London place name simply leads him on
to the next, we can clearly follow his method in making up a long and
meaningless speech which ironically apes the exchanges of reminiscences
between new acquaintances who want to break the ice between themselves
by recalling mutual friends with a maximum of circumstantial detail. So
transparent is the associative mechanism here that we are also fully aware
that Mick is malevolently enjoying himself at Davies's expense.

It is by an analogous use of associative linguistic structure that Pinter
indicates that a character is lying: here too the story is being made up as it
goes along, and often merely from the *sound* of the words; as in Solto's reply
to the question of how he got to Australia in *Night School*:

By sea. How do you think? I worked my passage. And
what a trip. I was only a pubescent. I killed a man with
my own hands, a six-foot-ten Lascar from Madagascar.
ANNIE: From Madagascar?
SOLTO: Sure. A Lascar.
MILLY: Alaska?
SOLTO: Madagascar.
Pause.
WALTER: It's all happened before.
SOLTO: And it'll happen again.

It is quite clear that Solto thought of Madagascar only because the term
Lascar suggested it. Walter's interjection, that it happened before, indicates
that he is fully aware of the spuriousness of the story and the intention
behind it, namely, the braggart's desire to impress. Hence by his remark he
shows himself unimpressed, while Solto, by insisting that it happened and
will happen again, feebly insists on his veracity, but without carrying any
conviction.

The braggart is a stock figure of comedy and has been from time im-
memorial; so, of course, have been the braggart's stories and lies. Here Pinter,
therefore, moves along very traditional lines; where his special talent shines
through, however, is in his ability to make the often very pathetic thought
processes behind the tall stories utterly transparent to the audience: these
liars are carried along, almost passively, by the limited range of their imagination, the paucity of possible associations which can lead them on from
one word to the next. When Walter, again in *Night School*, brags to Sally
about his success as a prison librarian, for example, he is, very much against
his will and better judgement, driven into a mention of rare manuscripts:

> Well, funny enough, I've had a good bit to do with rare manu-
> scripts in my time. I used to know a bloke who ran a business
> digging them up. . . . Rare manuscripts. Out of tombs. I used
> to give him a helping hand when I was on the loose. Very well
> paid it was, too. You see, they were nearly always attached to a
> corpse, these manuscripts, you had to lift up the pelvis bone with
> a pair of tweezers. Big tweezers. Can't leave fingerprints on a
> corpse, you see. Canon law.

(The germ of this speech is already contained in Pinter's early novel *The
Dwarfs*, where Pete tries to impress a girl during a party. In the passage in
Night School, however, the idea has been considerably, and brilliantly, developed and expanded.) It is only superficially that a speech like this one is
funny. On a deeper level it reveals an underprivileged individual's desperate
attempt to impress the girl, the mixture of ignorance and half-baked information with which his mind is stocked, the vagueness of his ideas. Rare
manuscripts to him suggest archaeology—archaeology, tombs—and somehow he has to invent for himself a way in which these two vague ideas can
be related: hence the suggestion that rare manuscripts are found in tombs.
Hence the association with skeletons; hence, again, the urge to mention one
of the few technical terms from anatomy he knows—"pelvis"—which again
leads to the association with the cliché of the soap opera involving an operation: it is here that tweezers are always mentioned. And this brings the
ex-convict Walter back to his own sphere: to explain the tweezers he gets
back to his own world, that of the petty thief who does not want to leave
fingerprints. To retrieve this lapse he has to take avoiding action into Canon
Law. . . . While it is unlikely that the audience will be wholly conscious of
the exact way in which such a chain of associations is built up, they can
certainly follow the main line of the underlying thought process and thus
partake in the *action* which this speech portrays, Walter's desperate attempt

on the one hand to establish his intellectual and social superiority and his equally desperate efforts, on the other, to extricate himself from the more and more difficult traps and pitfalls he creates for himself.

Always, in Pinter's world, personal inadequacy expresses itself in an inadequacy in coping with and using language. The inability to communicate, and to *communicate in the correct terms*, is felt by the characters as a mark of inferiority; that is why they tend to dwell upon and to stress the hard or unusual "educated" words they know. Solto, in the rodomontade quoted above, casually introduces the unusual, and to him no doubt highly refined term "pubescent," Walter talks about "Canon Law," "pelvis," "rare manuscripts"; Mick in *The Caretaker*, on his first confrontation with Davies, speaks of someone of whom the tramp reminds him, who had a *penchant* for nuts:

> Had a penchant for nuts. That's what it was. Nothing else but
> a penchant. Couldn't eat enough of them. Peanuts, walnuts, brazil
> nuts, monkey nuts, wouldn't touch a piece of fruit cake.

Note, again, the laying bare of the mechanism of the lie: the false circumstantial detail contained in the associative use of the names of different kinds of nuts. The introduction of the "refined" term *penchant*, however, serves to emphasize Mick's claim to superior education, intelligence and *savoir-faire*. It is, thus, equivalent to an *act of aggression*. Again and again veritable duels of this type develop among Pinter's characters. The memorable dispute about whether one says "light the kettle" or "light the gas" in *The Dumb Waiter* belongs to this category. Words like "penchant" and "pubescent" are proofs of superior general education. The use of technical terms and professional jargon, on the other hand, establishes the speaker's superiority in his own chosen field and gives him the advantages of belonging to a freemasonry, an inner circle of people who are able to exclude intruders and interlopers. The use of technical jargon thus corresponds to the enclosed rooms and protected spaces which Pinter's characters tend to covet and to defend against outsiders. When Mick finally turns against Davies and initiates the move which will expel him from the home he has been seeking, he overwhelms him with a demonstration of his ignorance of the skills he alleges Davies claimed when applying for the post of a caretaker in his house:

> I only told you because I understood you were an
> experienced first-class professional interior and exterior
> decorator.
> DAVIES: Now look here—
> MICK: You mean you wouldn't know how to fit teal-blue,

> copper and parchment linoleum squares and have those
> colours re-echoed in the walls?
> DAVIES: Now, look here, where'd you get—?
> MICK: You wouldn't be able to decorate out a table in afromosia
> teak veneer, an armchair in oatmeal tweed and a beech
> frame settee with a woven sea-grass seat?
> DAVIES: I never said that!
> MICK: Christ! I must have been under a false impression!
> DAVIES: I never said it!
> MICK: You're a bloody impostor, mate!

Davies's inability to comprehend the technical jargon of the interior decorator seals what, in effect, is his death sentence. In fact he had never directly claimed any such knowledge, but had merely tacitly nodded his approval when Mick, using the selfsame terms, had tempted him with the job of caretaker while outlining his grandiose plans for converting the derelict dwelling into a "penthouse." Incomprehension and the inability to express himself is clearly stated to be the reason for his loss of favour with Mick:

> Honest. I can take nothing you say at face value. Every word
> you speak is open to any number of different interpretations.
> Most of what you say is lies. You're violent, you're erratic, you're
> just completely unpredictable. You're nothing else but a wild
> animal, when you come down to it. You're a barbarian.

The ability to communciate is here equated with civilization, even the possession of a claim to being human. The loser in a contest about words and their meaning loses his claim to live. Power, the power over life or death, derives from the ability to make one's opponent accept the meaning of words chosen by the dominant partner. When Davies, earlier in *The Caretaker*, ventures to remark that Aston, Mick's brother, is "a bit of a funny bloke," Mick stares at him in indignant amazement:

> MICK: Funny? Why?
> DAVIES: Well . . . he's funny . . .
> MICK: What's funny about him?
> *Pause.*
> DAVIES: Not liking work.
> MICK: What's funny about that?
> DAVIES: Nothing.
> *Pause.*

MICK: I don't call it funny.
DAVIES: Nor me.

His surrender is both abject and complete. A disagreement about the meaning of a term has become a fundamental, existential contest of wills. Words, thus, are of vital importance. And yet, it is not so much the words themselves as the existential situations they conceal and reveal. It is not coincidence that the climactic turning point of *The Homecoming* arises from a "philosophical" discussion, Lenny's attempt to draw his brother Teddy into an argument about being and nonbeing, words and the realities behind them:

LENNY: Well, for instance, take a table. Philosophically
    speaking. What is it?
TEDDY: A table.
LENNY: Ah. You mean it's nothing else but a table. Well, some
    people would envy your certainty, wouldn't they, Joey?
    For instance, I've got a couple of friends of mine, we often
    sit round the Ritz Bar having a few liqueurs, and they are
    always saying things like that, you know, things like:
    Take a table, take it. All right, I say, *take* it, *take* a table,
    but once you've taken it, what you going to do with it?
    Once you've got hold of it, where you going to take it?
MAX: You'd probably sell it.
LENNY: You wouldn't get much for it.
JOEY: Chop it up for firewood.
    Lenny looks at him and laughs.
RUTH: Don't be too sure though. You've forgotten something.
    Look at me. I . . . move my leg. That's all it is. But I
    wear . . . underwear . . . which moves with me . . . it
    . . . captures your attention. Perhaps you misinterpret.
    The action is simple. It's a leg . . . moving. My lips
    move. Why don't you restrict . . . your observations to
    that? Perhaps the fact that they move is more significant
    . . . than the words which come through them. You must
    bear that . . . possibility . . . in mind.

Perhaps the fact that the lips move is more significant than the words which come through them! This key sentence not only touches the basis of Pinter's practice of the use of dramatic dialogue, it also reveals his fundamental philosophical attitude: his search, through and in spite of, an obsessive preoccupation with language, its nuances, its meaning, its beauty, for the area of reality that lies *behind* the use of language. It is not the word table that matters, but the way you *take* the table, how you *act* on it and how it *acts* on you, what it does to you. The lips that move are more significant, ultimately, than the words that come through them, the leg and the underwear which moves with it has more reality, because it is an action which creates an immediate response, than any of the polite words that a respectable professor's wife like Ruth might utter. Or, to put it differently, it matters little whether Mick's or Davies's interpretation of the word "funny" is the correct one, what is essential and existentially important is that Mick makes Davies accept *his* definition of the word's meaning.

Thus, again and again in Pinter's plays language becomes the medium through which a contest of wills is fought out, sometimes overtly as in the disputes about the correct expression to be used or about the correct meaning of a given word or phrase, sometimes beneath the surface of the explicit subject matter of the dialogue. The brainwashing of Stanley by Goldberg and McCann in *The Birthday Party* shows the transition from the one mode to the other with particular clarity; it opens with specific questions referring to Stanley's real situation:

> Why do you behave so badly, Webber? Why do you force that old man out to play chess?

Yet gradually the questions become more and more fantastic, more and more abstract, until in the end we are, indeed, made aware that it is the lips that are moving, and the rage with which they move, that matters rather than the words they utter. Nevertheless the words are of the utmost importance; not through their surface meaning, but through the colour and texture of their sound *and* their *associations* of meaning. At first Goldberg and McCann bombard Stanley with questions about specific crimes, which, however, are so contradictory that it is clear that he could not really have committed all of them: at one point he is asked:

> Why did you kill your wife?

A few lines later his crime is:

> Why did you never get married?

As the cross-examination proceeds, it becomes ever more obvious that it is an expression of Stanley's *general* feelings of guilt, of his tormentors' general conviction that he deserves punishment; the long list of venial and mortal sins, major and minor transgressions, which is unleashed upon poor Stanley—

You stuff yourself with dry toast.
You contaminate womankind.
Why don't you pay the rent?
Why do you pick your nose?
What about Ireland?

—covers the whole gamut of possible sources of guilt feelings: from embarrassment over social gaffes (picking one's nose), collective national guilt feelings about crimes committed by one's country (Ireland for the Englishman Stanley Webber), minor lapses (such as eating too much toast) to the major sins of lechery and even the worst of all, cheating at the national sport:

Who watered the wicket in Melbourne?

until it culminates in the final, existential question of why the chicken crossed the road, and which came first, the chicken or the egg—in other words, why Stanley has the effrontery of existing, of being alive at all. The proliferation of images, grotesquely juxtaposed and subtly intensified, establishes this long scene as a kind of poem, a structure of images which constitutes a set of variations on a basic theme. The chief character of the play is thrown, as it were, into a whirlpool of language which batters him into insensitivity.

(Ten years after Pinter wrote *The Birthday Party*, Peter Handke, a young protagonist of the theatrical avant-garde in Germany, achieved considerable success with a new kind of dramatic spectacle which he called "Sprechstücke" (word plays); these consist of long structures of pure language uttered by speakers who do not represent any specific characters, but which, by confronting the audience with permutations of words and associations on a given theme (the future; cries for help; insults; or, indeed, the sources of guilt feelings) set up linguistic fields of force, from which each member of the audience must, willy-nilly, assemble his own personal experience of hope, helplessness, rage or guilt. Pinter not only anticipated this "new" experimental form, but also demonstrated how it could be integrated and made to work within a more traditional framework of drama.)

Brilliant as the brainwashing scene in *The Birthday Party* is, Pinter's use of language became far subtler in his later plays. When Lenny first meets Ruth in *The Homecoming* he tells her two long, and seemingly gratuitous, stories. As in *The Birthday Party*'s brainwashing scene, these are linguistic structures designed to evoke feelings of guilt and terror in the listener; but they are far more subtly orchestrated, far less obviously abstract *tours de force*. Having just met Ruth late at night and alone in his house, Lenny at first engages her in the usual small talk. Then suddenly out of a speech about

her visit to Venice and his feeling that he might have seen Venice had he
served in the last war, he confronts her with a clearly erotic proposition:

> Do you mind if I hold your hand?
> RUTH: Why?
> LENNY: Just a touch.
> *He stands and goes to her.*
> Just a tickle.
> RUTH: Why?
> *He looks down at her.*
> LENNY: I'll tell you why.
> *Slight pause.*

Lenny then launches into his first long story, which seems totally unrelated
to the question he promised to answer—namely, why he wants to touch
Ruth. The story starts on a formal linguistic level, almost like the opening
sentences of a novel—

> One night, not too long ago, one night down by the docks, I was
> standing alone under an arch, watching all the men jibbing the
> boom, out in the harbour, and playing about with the yardarm.

Note the use of technical terms of nautical language as an indication of
expertise, of being an insider! Ruth and the audience will now expect to
hear that Lenny (whose occupation is a mystery) might turn out to have
something to do with the sea. But at this point the story—and the language—
suddenly change gear—

> when a certain lady came up to me and made a certain proposal.

Now we are in the terminology of the British popular press when it deals,
as politely and respectably as is possible under the circumstances, with sexual
matters and above all sex crimes:

> This lady had been searching for me for days. She'd lost track
> of my whereabouts. However, the fact was she eventually caught
> up with me, and when she caught up with me she made me this
> certain proposal. Well, this proposal wasn't entirely out of order
> and normally I would have subscribed to it. I mean I would have
> subscribed to it in the normal course of events. The only trouble
> was—

and here the language again enters, abruptly, another sphere altogether—

The only trouble was she was falling apart with the pox.

This is another field of technical jargon: the professional talk of pimps and prostitutes. Lenny has shown his hand: he has indicated that this is his world. What is more: he goes on to discuss, very dispassionately and coolly, his desire to kill the girl there and then—

> and the fact is, that as killings go, it would have been a simple matter, nothing to it.

—and concludes the story with his decision, *not* to kill her—

> But . . . in the end I thought . . . Aaah, why go to all the bother . . . you know, getting rid of the corpse and all that, getting youself into a state of tension. So I just gave her another belt in the nose and a couple of turns of the boot and sort of left it at that.

Again it is the switching from the polite language of the newspaper crime report to the brutal vernacular of the criminal himself which makes the point. In answer to Ruth's question why he made her an erotic proposal, Lenny has told her that being engaged in the business of prostitution, and being in a position to reject such proposals from other girls, he feels himself entitled to make such claims, and that, indeed, such claims should be regarded as an honour by the women to whom they are addressed. Ruth's reaction shows that she has understood the import of the story only too well. Displaying no surprise whatever, she instinctively, or deliberately, falls into the same technical jargon.

> RUTH: How did you know she was diseased?
> LENNY: How did I know?
> *Pause.*
> I decided she was.
> *Silence.*
> You and my brother are newly-weds, are you?

Having, by her lack of surprise and the technical language of her question, revealed that she comes from the same world, Ruth is, in Lenny's answer, sharply reminded by him that his power over his girls is absolute. If he decides that a girl is diseased, then she is diseased. The point is made. Lenny can change the subject and return to polite small talk. But it is merely a short break in the contest of wills. Again, to establish his determination to be brutal to women, be they helpless and old, Lenny tells his second long

story about the lady who asked him to move her mangle, while he was
employed to clear the snow in the streets on a winter morning, but failed
to give him a helping hand with the heavy object:

> So after a few minutes I said to her, now look here, why don't
> you stuff mangle up your arse? Anyway, I said, they're out of
> date, you want to get a spin-drier. I had a good mind to give her
> a workover there and then, but as I was feeling jubilant with the
> snow-clearing I just gave her a short-arm jab to the belly and
> jumped on a bus outside. Excuse me, shall I take this ashtray out
> of your way?

The narration of a brutal assault on an old woman is directly linked to the
seemingly trivial questions about the ashtray. But in fact the ashtray and
the glass which stand beside it become the focus for the first direct confrontation between Ruth and Lenny. She does not want to move the ashtray
and she wants to keep the glass as she is still thirsty. And Ruth, having been
told of Lenny's capacity for being brutal to women, and having taken it all
in, openly challenges him:

> If you take the glass . . . I'll take you.

And she goes over to the attack:

> *She picks up the glass and lift it towards him.*
> RUTH: Have a sip. Go on. Have a sip from my glass.
> *He is still.*
> Sit on my lap. Take a long cool sip.
> *She pats her lap. Pause.*
> *She stands, moves to him with the glass.*
> Put your head back and open your mouth.
> LENNY: Take that glass away from me.
> RUTH: Lie on the floor. Go on. I'll pour it down your throat.
> LENNY: What are you doing, making me some kind of
> proposal?
> *She laughs shortly, drains the glass.*

Ruth has turned the tables completely. She has become the girl who makes
a proposal to Lenny; but Lenny fails to do to her what he had boasted he
had done to the girl who had made him that certain proposal.

The audience, witnessing the play for the first time will, of course, not
be consciously aware of *all* the information which the playwright has, subtly,
supplied in the shifts of linguistic levels, the echoing and reechoing of key-
words (e.g., "proposal"); to them the strange night scene with its long and

seemingly pointless narrative passages and the sudden contest of wills must seem "enigmatic," provocatively suggestive but barely penetrable. Dramatically this is an advantage, because it generates one of the most important elements in all drama—suspense. Yet, as in the best detective fiction, the clues are all provided, and with scrupulous fairness; they are present in the language itself which lets us see through it into the depths of the unspoken thoughts and emotions of the two characters: Lenny propositions Ruth because he has sensed that she is like the girls with whom he deals in his profession. When she asks *why* he has propositioned her, he tells her, by gradually falling into the brutal trade language of the pimp, what he is and—by implication—what he thinks she may well be. And by her reaction—or rather the absence of a shocked reaction, the acceptance of a man who uses that kind of language as a matter of course—she clearly indicates that she does in fact belong to that same world. Hence Ruth's acceptance of the role of a prostitute when it is offered to her towards the end of the play, which tends to shock audiences so deeply, has already been anticipated in his scene of her first confrontation with Lenny. And so has the sovereign, disdainfully businesslike attitude with which she settles the terms of her new life by driving an exceedingly hard bargain: for in that first contest of wills she had shown herself fully Lenny's equal in ruthlessness.

In fact, if one analyses Pinter's work closely, one will find that behind the apparently random rendering of the colloquial vernacular, there lies a rigorous economy of means: each word is essential to the total structure and decisively contributes to the ultimate, overall effect aimed at. In this respect also Pinter's use of language is that of a poet; there are no redundant words in true poetry, no empty patches, no mere fill-ins. Pinter's dramatic writing has the density of texture of true poetry.

That is why—as in poetry the caesura, as in music the pause—silences play such a large and essential part in Pinter's dialogue. Pinter uses two different terms for the punctuation of his dialogue by passages without speech: "Pause" and "Silence." In the above example, which has been analysed in some detail, when at the end of Lenny's first narration, Ruth asks how he knew the girl in question was diseased (and thus reveals her lack of surprise and familiarity with the vocabulary) Lenny's reaction is:

> How did I know?
> *Pause.*
> I decided she was.
> *Silence.*
> You and my brother are newlyweds, are you?

The repetition of the question, "how did I know" shows Lenny's surprise at Ruth's reaction; he can hardly, as yet, believe that she would react in so matter-of-fact a way. The "pause" bridges the time he needs to take in the whole import of that reaction and to think out his reply. The "silence" after his reply and before he changes the subject indicates the much deeper caesura of the end of that section of the conversation. When Pinter asks for a *pause*, therefore, he indicates that intense thought processes are continuing, that unspoken tensions are mounting, whereas *silences* are notations for the end of a movement, the beginning of another, as between the movements of a symphony.

The pauses and silences in Pinter's plays are the answer to Len's question in the novel *The Dwarfs* when he was speaking about those poets who climb from word to word like stepping stones:

> What do they do when they come to a line with no words in it
> at all?

For the answer to that question is that *drama* is a kind of poetry which *can* find room for the emotional charge of the unspoken line: What speaks on the stage is the situation itself, the characters who confront each other in silence, what has gone before and the expectation, the suspense as to what will happen next. Pinter's pauses and silences are thus often the climaxes of his plays, the still centres of the storm, the nuclei of tension around which the whole action is structured: there is the "long silence" at the end of *The Caretaker* when Davies's pleading for permission to remain in Aston's room elicits no answer. This "long silence" is the death of hope for the old man, Aston's refusal to forgive him, his expulsion from the warmth of a home— death. But, as the curtain falls before he is seen to leave, it may also be the long silence before that final word of forgiveness is pronounced: the "line with no words in it" thus has all the ambiguity and complexity of true poetry and it is also a metaphor, an image of overwhelming power.

Likewise, at the close of *The Collection* after Bill's "final" confession, his last version of the incident with James's wife, Stella, namely, that nothing happened between them at all, Pinter calls for a "long silence," after which James leaves the house. And then the silence continues as Harry and Bill remain sitting, facing each other. That silence contains an image of the despair and horror of their mutual dependence, above all of Bill's final failure to free himself from Harry's domination. As the light fades on that image, James is seen returning to his own home and confronting his wife:

> JAMES: You didn't do anything, did you?
> *Pause.*

He wasn't in your room. You just talked about it, in the
lounge.
Pause.
That's the truth, isn't it?
Pause.
You just sat and talked about what you would do if you
went to your room. That's what you did.
Pause.
Didn't you?
Pause.
That's the truth . . . isn't it?
*Stella looks at him neither confirming nor denying. Her face is
friendly, sympathetic.*

Stella's silence, her refusal to confirm or deny the story, is, in the true
dramatic sense, an *action*, the pause which echoes each of James's questions
is a line of dialogue, it is also a poetic image of one human being's mystery
and impenetrability for another. This, it must again be stressed, has nothing
to do with man's *inability* to communciate with his fellow man: what is being
demonstrated is man's—or this woman's—*unwillingness* to communicate, and
indeed, her partner's inability ever to be certain that, whether she speaks or
remains silent, he can get hold of the real, the inner, personal, truth of the
matter.

That silence which is a *refusal* to communcate is one of the dominant
images of Pinter's plays: from Bert's nonresponsiveness to Rose in his first
play *The Room* to Beth's inability or unwillingness to hear, and to respond
to, what Duff tells her in *Landscape*.

There is another speechlessness, however, in Pinter's work, the speechlessness of annihilation, of total collapse: we find it in Stanley's inarticulate
"uh-gughh" and caaahhh" at the end of *The Birthday Party*, in Edward's silent
acceptance of the matchseller's tray in the closing moment of *A Slight Ache*,
in Disson's catatonic collapse at the close of *Tea Party*. This, also, is the
silence which gives its title to the play *Silence*—the silence of the gradual
fading of memory, the gradual, inevitable dissolution of human personality
itself.

To be filled, to be meaningful, Pinter's silences and pauses have to be
meticulously *prepared*: only if the audience knows the possible alternative
answers to a question can the absence of a reply acquire meaning and dramatic
impact; only because we know what Disson might want to say—and indeed
the way in which he is torn between the conflicting desires and fears he is

unable to keep under control—are we moved by his inability to speak. Thus the effectiveness of the pauses and silences is, in Pinter's technique, the direct consequence of the density of texture of his writing: each syllable and each silence is part of an overall design, all portions of which are totally integrated; another way to put this would be to say that Pinter's writing is of the utmost economy, there are no redundant parts in it. It is the economy by which a door, a simple, ordinary door, can become a source of nameless fear and menace, merely because the character in the room has been shown to dread the intrusion of the outside world: the economy of means through which a character who has been kept silent through most of the play can cause an effect of overwhelming surprise by suddenly starting to speak; the economy of words which can invest the most threadbare cliché with hidden poetic meaning.

Teddy's departure in *The Homecoming* might be cited as a telling, final example of this supreme economy of Pinter' dramatic technique. Ruth, Teddy's wife, has consented to stay behind with the family and to become a prostitute. Teddy is returning to America alone. He has said goodbye to all the men in the room. He has not spoken to Ruth. He goes to the door. Then Ruth speaks: she calls him—"Eddie."

Throughout the play Ruth has never addressed Teddy by his name. Talking to the others she has referred to him, as they have, as Teddy. The fact that she now calls him by a different name, the name which no doubt was the one she used when they were alone, thus acquires a particular force.

Teddy turns.

Quite clearly he feels that the use of a name which Ruth regarded as a part of their intimacy in earlier times may yet indicate that she has changed her mind, that she may yet come with him. But having turned, and having waited, he is greeted with silence. Pinter indicates a *pause*. Then Ruth merely says: "Don't become a stranger."

"Don't become a stranger" is a cliché, an idiom without any emotional force. It is what one says to a casual acquaintance after the holiday is over, the cruise has come to an end; if one were to explain the phrase in a dictionary of idioms one would translate it with no more than: we might meet again: or: see you some time. This, clearly, is also how Teddy understands it. For he goes and shuts the front door. Pinter indicates a "silence." But in that silence, which concludes Teddy's visit, which sets a full stop to his appearance in the play and probably in the lives of the other characters, surely there will also echo something of the *literal* meaning of that phrase "don't become a stranger," rather like a last despairing lament of a wife for the husband she has now lost, who has, in fact, at that very moment become a stranger to her.

Only five words, only eight syllables are actually spoken in that whole passage: "Eddie—Don't become a stranger." But through the surprise use of a name, through a pregnant pause, and an utterly final silence, and through the subtle ambiguity of a phrase which is both a weak cliché and yet carries a literal meaning of deep, tragic impact, Pinter has put a wealth of drama, psychological profundity, suspense, irony and pathos into those eight syllables.

Such economy and subtlety in the use of language, such density of subtext beneath the sparseness of the text itself, is surely the hallmark of a real master of the craft of dialogue.

Chronology

1930   Harold Pinter born in Hackney, London, only child of an East End Jewish tailor.

1946   Publishes an essay on James Joyce in the *Hackney Downs School Magazine*.

1947   Publishes two poems, "Dawn" and "O Beloved Maidens," and an essay, "Blood Sports," in the same magazine.

1948   Joins Royal Academy of Dramatic Art.

1949–57   Conscientious objector of National Service.

1950   Publishes two poems in *Poetry London*. Acts in radio play, *Focus on Football Pools*.

1951   Studies at Central School of Speech and Drama. Appears with McMaster's theater company, touring Ireland.

1953   Acts in Donald Wolfit's productions at King's Theatre, Hammersmith.

1954   Under stage name of David Barron, acts with provincial theater companies. Also works as waiter, doorman, dishwasher, and door-to-door salesman.

1956   Marries actress Vivien Merchant.

1957   *The Room* given student production at the Bristol University Drama Department and is subsequently produced in a student drama competition at the Bristol Old Vic sponsored by the *Sunday Times*.

1958   Pinter's son Daniel born. *The Birthday Party* has an unsuccessful one-week run in London.

1959   *The Dumb Waiter* produced in Frankfurt. Two skits, "Trouble in the Works" and "The Black and the White," presented at *The New Lyric Revue* at Hammersmith. *A Slight Ache* is broadcast on the BBC's Third Programme. A short story, "The Examination," published in *Prospect*.

1960   First English production of *The Room* and *The Dumb Waiter* at the Hampstead Theatre Club. *A Night Out* broadcast on the BBC Third Programme. Pinter plays Mick in the successful West End production of *The Caretaker*. A prose version of "Black and White" is published in *The Spectator*, July 1. *The Birthday Party* is performed at Actors Workshop, San Francisco. *The Dwarfs*, adapted from an early unpublished novel, is broadcast on the BBC Third Programme, December 2.

1961   *The Collection* televised by Associated Rediffusion Television.

1962   Pinter codirects (with Peter Hall) a production of *The Collection* by the Royal Shakespeare Company.

1963   *The Lover* receives the Guild of British Television Producers and Directors Award.

1964   Pinter directs Royal Shakespeare Company's production of *The Birthday Party*. Five radio plays, "Applicant," "Dialogue for Three," "Interview," "That's All," and "That's Your Trouble," are broadcast on the BBC Third Programme. *The Servant* receives the British Screenwriters' Guild Award and the New York Film Critics Best Writing Award.

1965   *The Homecoming* staged at the Aldwych Theatre, London. *Tea Party* is televised by BBC-1 in England and Europe. *The Pumpkin Eater* (screenplay by Pinter from Penelope Mortimer's novel) recieves the British Film Academy Award.

1966   Made a Commander of the Order of the British Empire on the Queen's Birthday Honours List.

1967   Plays Scott in a television production of *The Basement*. Directs Robert Shaw's play, *The Man in the Glass Booth*. *Accident* (screenplay by Pinter) receives the Cannes Jury Prize as well as a National Board of Review Award. *The Homecoming* receives an Antoinette Perry (Tony) Award and the New York Drama Critics' Circle Award.

1968   *Landscape* is broadcast on the BBC Third Programme. Publishes a memoir, *Mac*, and a collection of *Poems*.

1969   *Landscape* and *Silence* are staged at the Aldwych Theatre.

1971   *Old Times* produced at the Aldwych Theatre. *The Go-Between* receives Cannes Film Festival Award for best picture. Honorary degree conferred on Pinter by the University of Birmingham.

1973   Pinter appointed Associate Director of the National Theatre. *Monologue* televised.

1975   *No Man's Land* produced at the National Theatre.

1978   *Betrayal* produced at the National Theatre. *Poems and Prose 1949–1977* published.

1980   *The Hothouse* produced at the Hampstead Theater, London. *Family Voices* broadcast on BBC radio. After divorce from Vivien Merchant, Pinter marries Lady Antonia Fraser, the writer.

1981   *The French Lieutenant's Woman*, a film based on Pinter's adaptation of John Fowles's novel, released. *Family Voices* staged at the National Theatre.

1982   *Victoria Station*, *A Kind of Alaska*, *Family Voices* in a triple bill at the National Theatre. The three plays are published in a collection entitled *Other Places*.

1983   *Players* produced at the National Theatre.

1984   An early play, *One for the Road*, published in *The New York Review of Books*.

1985   Film *Turtle Diary*, screenplay by Pinter, released.

Contributors

HAROLD BLOOM, Sterling Professor of the Humanities at Yale University, is the author of *The Anxiety of Influence*, *Poetry and Repression*, and many other volumes of literary criticism. His forthcoming study, *Freud: Transference and Authority*, attempts a full-scale reading of all of Freud's major writings. A MacArthur Prize Fellow, he is general editor of five series of literary criticism published by Chelsea House.

BERT O. STATES is Professor of Drama at the University of California, Santa Barbara, and the author of *Irony and Drama*.

RAYMOND WILLIAMS, Judith F. Wilson Professor of Drama at Cambridge University, is the most influential of British Marxist literary critics. His books include *Culture and Society*, *The Long Revolution*, and *The Country and the City*.

JOHN RUSSELL BROWN is Professor of Theatre Arts at the State University of New York, Stony Brook, and the author of *Theatre Language*.

JAMES EIGO is a writer and playwright based in New York.

AUSTIN E. QUIGLEY is Associate Professor of English at the University of Virginia and the author of *The Pinter Problem*.

BARBARA KREPS is Assistant Professor of English at the University of Pisa, Italy, and has written on Donne and Shakespeare.

GUIDO ALMANSI is Professor of English and Comparative Literature at the University of East Anglia. He is the author of *Harold Pinter* (with Simon Henderson) and *Montale: The Private Language of Poetry* (with Bruce Merry) as well as studies of parody, Boccaccio and Shakespeare, and obscene literature.

ENOCH BRATER is Professor of English at the University of Michigan, Ann Arbor and has written widely on modern drama.

THOMAS F. VAN LAAN is Professor of English at Rutgers University and the author of *The Idiom of Drama* and *Role-Playing in Shakespeare*.

ELIN DIAMOND, Assistant Professor of English at the University of Rutgers, New Brunswick, is the author of *Pinter's Comic Play* and is working on a book on feminist theory and plays by women.

MARTIN ESSLIN, formerly Head of Radio Drama for the BBC, currently is Professor of Drama at Stanford University. In addition to his study of Pinter, his books include *The Theatre of the Absurd, Brecht: The Man and His Work*, and *Reflections: Essays on Modern Theatre*.

Bibliography

Almansi, Guido, and Simon Henderson. *Harold Pinter*. London: Methuen, 1983.

Baker, William, and Ely Tabachnick. *Harold Pinter*. Edinburgh: Oliver & Boyd, 1973.

Bock, Hedwig. "Harold Pinter: The Room as Symbol." In *Essays on Contemporary British Drama*, edited by Hedwig Bock and Albert Wertheim, 171–84. Munich: Max Hueber Verlag, 1981.

Boulton, James T. "Harold Pinter: *The Caretaker* and Other Plays." *Modern Drama* 6 (1963): 131–40.

Bovie, Palmer. "Seduction: The Amphitryon Theme from Plautus to Pinter." *The Minnesota Review* 7, nos. 3–4 (1967): 304–13.

———. "Time and Memory in Pinter's Screenplay." *Comparative Drama* 13 (1979): 121–26.

Braunmuller, Albert R. "Harold Pinter: The Metamorphosis of Memory." In *Essays on Contemporary British Drama*, edited by Hedwig Bock and Albert Wertheim, 155–70. Munich: Max Hueber Verlag, 1981.

Brown, John R. "Dialogue in Pinter and Others." *Critical Quarterly* 7 (1965): 225–43.

———. "Mr. Pinter's Shakespeare." *Critical Quarterly* 5 (1963): 251–65.

———. *Theatre Language*. London: Lane, 1972.

———, ed. *Modern British Dramatists*. Englewood Cliffs, N.J.: Prentice-Hall, 1968.

Bryden, Ronald. "Pinter's New Pacemaker." *The Observer* (London), 6 June 1971.

———. "A Stink of Pinter." *New Statesman*, 11 June 1965, 928.

Burghardt, Lorraine Hall. "Game Playing in Three by Pinter." *Modern Drama* 17 (1974): 363–75.

Burkman, Katherine. *The Dramatic World of Harold Pinter: Its Basis in Ritual*. Columbus: Ohio State University Press, 1971.

Callen, A. "Comedy and Passion in the Plays of Harold Pinter." *Forum for Modern Language Studies* 4 (1968): 299–305.

Carpenter, Charles. "The Absurdity of Dread: Pinter's *The Dumb Waiter*." *Modern Drama* 16 (1973): 279–85.

Cohn, Ruby. "The Absurdly Absurd: Avatars of Godot." *Comparative Literature Studies* 2 (1965): 233–40.

———. "Words Working Overtime: *Endgame* and *No Man's Land*." *Yearbook of English Studies* 9 (1979): 181–203.

Colby, Douglas. *As the Curtain Rises: On Contemporary British Drama 1966–1976*. Rutherford, N.J.: Fairleigh Dickinson University Press, 1978.

Dawick, John. " 'Punctuation' and Patterning in *The Homecoming*." *Modern Drama* 14 (1971): 37–46.

Dennis, Nigel. "Pintermania." *The New York Review of Books*, 17 December 1970, 21–22.

Diamond, Elin. "Pinter's *Betrayal* and the Comedy of Manners." *Modern Drama* 25 (1980): 238–45.

Dukore, Bernard F. "The Pinter Collection." *Educational Theatre Journal* 26 (March 1974): 81–85.

———. *Where Laughter Stops: Pinter's Tragicomedy*. Columbia: University of Missouri Press, 1976.

Esslin, Martin. *Pinter: A Study of His Plays*. London: Methuen, 1976.

———. "Pinter Translated: On International Non-communication." *Encounter* 30, no. 3 (1968): 45–47.

Firth, J. R., "The Tongues of Men." In *The Tongues of Men and Speech*. London: Oxford University Press, 1966.

Gabbard, Lucinda Paquet. *The Dream Structure of Pinter's Plays: A Psychoanalytic Approach*. Rutherford, N.J.: Fairleigh Dickinson University Press, 1976.

Gale, Steven. *Butter's going up:* A critical analysis of Harold Pinter's work. Durham, N.C.: Duke University Press, 1977.

Ganz, Arthur. *Realms of the Self*. New York: New York University Press, 1980.

———, ed. *Pinter: A Collection of Critical Essays*. Englewood Cliffs, N.J.: Prentice-Hall, 1972.

Hayman, Ronald. *Harold Pinter*. New York: Frederick Ungar, 1973.

Hughes, Alan. "Myth and Memory in Pinter's *Old Times*." *Modern Drama* 17 (1974): 467–76.

Jones, John Bush. "Stasis as Structure in Pinter's *No Man's Land*." *Modern Drama* 19 (1976): 291–304.

Kaufman, Michael W. "Actions That a Man Might Play: Pinter's *The Birthday Party*." *Modern Drama* 16 (1973): 167–78.

Kennedy, Andrew. *Dramatic Dialogue*. Cambridge: Cambridge University Press, 1983.

———. "Natural, Mannered, and Parodic Dialogue." *Yearbook of English Studies* 9 (1979): 22–54.

———. *Six Dramatists in Search of a Language*. Cambridge: Cambridge University Press, 1975.

Kerr, Walter. *Harold Pinter*. New York: Columbia University Press, 1967.

King, Noel. "Pinter's Progress." *Modern Drama* 23 (1980): 246–57.

Kitchin, Laurence. *Drama in the Sixties*. London: Faber & Faber, 1966.

Knight, G. Wilson. "The Kitchen Sink." *Encounter* 21, no. 6 (1963): 48–54.

Lahr, John. *A Casebook on Harold Pinter's* The Homecoming. New York: Grove Press, 1970.

———. "The Language of Silence." *Evergreen Review* 13, no. 64 (March 1969): 53–55, 82–90.

———. "Pinter the Spaceman." *Evergreen Review* 12, no. 55 (1968): 49–52, 87–90.

Marowitz, Charles. " 'Pinterism' Is Maximum Tension through Minimum Information." *The New York Times*, 1 October 1967.

Martineau, Stephen. "Pinter's *Old Times:* The Memory Game." *Modern Drama* 16 (1973): 287–97.

Morrison, Kristin. *Canters and Chronicles.* Chicago: University of Chicago Press, 1983.

———. "Pinter and the New Irony." *Quarterly Journal of Speech* 5 (1969): 388–93.

Quigley, Austin E. *The Pinter Problem.* Princeton: Princeton University Press, 1975.

Rodway, Alan. *English Comedy, Its Role and Nature from Chaucer to the Present Day.* Berkeley and Los Angeles: University of California Press, 1975.

Smith, Leslie. "Pinter the Player." *Modern Drama* 22 (1979): 249–63.

Storch, R. F. "Harold Pinter's Happy Families." *The Massachusetts Review* 8 (1967): 703–12.

Sykes, Alrene. *Harold Pinter.* St. Lucia, Australia: Queensland University Press, 1970.

Taylor, John Russell. *Anger and After.* London: Methuen, 1962.

Trussler, Simon. *The Plays of Harold Pinter.* London: Victor Gollancz, 1973.

Vannier, Jean. "Theatre of Language." *Tulane Drama Review* 7, no. 3 (1963): 180–86.

Williams, Raymond. *Drama from Ibsen to Brecht.* London: Chatto & Windus, 1968.

Walker, Augusta. "Messages from Pinter." *Modern Drama* 10 (1967): 1–10.

Wardle, Irving. "Comedy of Menace." *Encore* 5 (1958): 28–33.

Wray, P. "Pinter's Dialogue: The Play on Words." *Modern Drama* 13 (1971): 418–22.

Acknowledgments

"Pinter's *Homecoming*: The Shock of Nonrecognition" by Bert O. States from *The Hudson Review* 21, no. 3 (Autumn 1968), © 1968 by The Hudson Review, Inc. Reprinted by permission.

"*The Birthday Party*: Harold Pinter" by Raymond Williams from *Drama from Ibsen to Brecht* by Raymond Williams, © 1952, 1968 by Raymond Williams. Reprinted by permission of the author, Chatto and Windus Ltd., and Oxford University Press.

"Words and Silence: *The Birthday Party*" (originally entitled "Harold Pinter, Words and Silence: *The Birthday Party* and Other Plays") by John Russell Brown from *Theatre Language: A Study of Arden, Osborne, Pinter and Wesker* by John Russell Brown, © 1972 by John Russell Brown. Reprinted by permission of the author, Taplinger Publishing Co., Inc., and Allen Lane, The Penguin Press Ltd.

"Pinter's *Landscape*" by James Eigo from *Modern Drama* 16, no. 2 (September 1973), © 1973 by the University of Toronto, Graduate Centre for the Study of Drama. Reprinted by permission of *Modern Drama*.

"*The Room*" by Austin E. Quigley from *The Pinter Problem* by Austin E. Quigley, © 1975 by Princeton University Press. Reprinted by permission of Princeton University Press.

"Time and Harold Pinter's Possible Realities: Art as Life, and Vice Versa" by Barbara Kreps from *Modern Drama* 22, no. 1 (March 1979), © 1979 by the University of Toronto, Graduate Centre for the Study of Drama. Reprinted by permission of *Modern Drama*.

"Harold Pinter's Idiom of Lies" by Guido Almansi from *Contemporary English Drama* (Stratford-Upon-Avon Series 19), edited by C. W. E. Bigsby, © 1981 by Edward Arnold (Publishers) Ltd., London. Reprinted by permission.

"Cinematic Fidelity and the Forms of Pinter's *Betrayal*" by Enoch Brater from *Modern Drama* 24, no. 4 (December 1981), © 1981 by the University of Toronto, Graduate Centre for the Study of Drama. Reprinted by permission of *Modern Drama*.

"*The Dumb Waiter*: Pinter's Play with the Audience" by Thomas F. Van Laan from *Modern Drama* 24, no. 4 (December 1981), © 1981 by the University of Toronto,

Graduate Centre for the Study of Drama. Reprinted by permission of *Modern Drama*.

"Parody Play in Pinter" by Elin Diamond from *Modern Drama* 25, no. 4 (December 1982), © 1982 by the University of Toronto, Graduate Centre for the Study of Drama. Reprinted by permission of *Modern Drama*.

"Language and Silence" by Martin Esslin from *Pinter the Playwright* by Martin Esslin, © 1970, 1973, 1977, 1982 by Martin Esslin. Reprinted by permission of the author and Methuen & Co., Ltd., London.

Index